THE FUNDRAISING SERIES

Corporate Fundraising

Editor *Valerie Morton*

Third edition

The fundraising series
Community Fundraising Harry Brown (editor)
Major Donor Fundraising Margaret M Holman, Lucy Sargent
Fundraising Databases Peter Flory
Fundraising Strategy Redmond Mullin
Legacy Fundraising Sebastian Wilberforce (editor)
Trust Fundraising Anthony Clay (editor)
Marketing Strategy Peter Maple
Capital Campaigns Trudy Hayden

Published by
The Directory of Social Change   Tel 08450 77 77 07
24 Stephenson Way   Fax 020 7391 4804
London   e-mail: publications@dsc.org.uk
NW1 2DP

Customer services Tel 08450 77 77 07 from whom further copies and a full publications list are available.

The Directory of Social Change is a Registered Charity no. 800517

Original text and cover design by Eugenie Dodd Typographics, London
Typeset by Keystroke, Wolverhampton
Printed and bound by Page Bros., Norwich

British Library Cataloguing in Publication Data
A catalogue record for this book is available from the British Library

ISBN-13 978 1 903991 88 6

Contents

The fundraising series vi
About the authors vii
Foreword xiv
Introduction and acknowledgements
Valerie Morton xv

PART 1   **Background and best practice 1**

CHAPTER ONE   The evolution of true corporate partnerships 3
                  Catherine Sermon

CHAPTER TWO   What is corporate social responsibility? 12
                  Mark Line

CHAPTER THREE   How companies support charities 21
                  Laura Baynham-Hughes

CHAPTER FOUR   Developing new business 30
                  Josephine Job

CHAPTER FIVE   Developing and managing corporate partnerships
                  in the 21st century 38
                  Andrew Peel

CHAPTER SIX   Getting the measure of corporate community
                  investment 47
                  Ita McMahon and Mike Tuffrey

CHAPTER SEVEN   Take it or leave it – corporate fundraising ethics 57
                  Ian MacQuillin

PART 2   **Case studies from corporate and charity perspectives 67**

CHAPTER EIGHT   Small charity – big success story – a case study from the Foundation for the Study of Infant Deaths 69
Sara Bowcutt and Catherine Bennett

CHAPTER NINE   EDF Energy – managing our impacts on the community 77
Alison Braybrooks

CHAPTER TEN   Brand synergy on the beach – a case study from RNLI and Wall's 86
Philippa Thompson

CHAPTER ELEVEN   Integrating corporate fundraising into an overall fundraising strategy – a case study of TreeHouse 93
Susan Beck

CHAPTER TWELVE   Ethical policies – a case study of Diabetes UK 103
Helen Hirons

CHAPTER THIRTEEN   The pitching process – BAE Systems 109
James Hayward

CHAPTER FOURTEEN   Marks & Spencer and Breakthrough Breast Cancer: no brief encounter – a case study in real partnership 116
Laurie Boult and Rachael Reeve

CHAPTER FIFTEEN   Managing a charity of the year campaign – a case study of HBOS 123
Joan Hemmery

CHAPTER SIXTEEN   United for UNICEF – a case study of a winning partnership 133
Beth Nicholls

CHAPTER SEVENTEEN   British Institute for Brain Injured Children (BIBIC) and IPC Media – a charity of the year partnership in the media industry 144
Jill Taylor and Taryn Barclay

PART 3   **Appendices 151**

APPENDIX ONE   Legal and tax issues 153
Anne-Marie Piper

APPENDIX TWO   Template for a corporate fundraising strategy 175
Andrew Peel and Carla Miller

APPENDIX THREE   An ethical framework for accepting or rejecting
corporate support 184
Ian MacQuillin

APPENDIX FOUR   Sources for corporate information 188
Robin Jones

INDEX 203

The Fundraising series

Fundraising evolves within a constantly changing fiscal and societal framework. The environment in turn influences the way in which funds are raised and how fundraising is conducted. Fundraising techniques and practice also evolve in response to the changing fiscal and societal environment. In order for fundraisers to be effective it is vital that they are a step ahead of the game. Successful fundraisers identify future trends, anticipate demand and develop new techniques to meet it.

The Charities Aid Foundation (CAF), Institute of Fundraising and Directory of Social Change (DSC) fundraising series seeks to address the full range of fundraising activity and techniques in one series. Each successive volume seeks to address one key element in the spectrum of fundraising techniques. As fundraising techniques evolve and develop, new titles in the series are added to and old ones revised.

The titles are intended as texts that encourage and debate fundraising within a professional framework – written and used by academics and practitioners alike. Each title seeks to explore the fundraising activity within its historical, ethical and theoretical context, relate it to current fundraising practice as well as guide future strategy.

The Institute of Fundraising is well placed to assist in the development and production of this series; without the support, assistance and expertise of its members and their colleagues, the series would not be possible. I thank all those who have contributed and continue to contribute to the most comprehensive fundraising series available today.

Megan Pacey
Director of Policy and Campaigns
Institute of Fundraising

About the authors

Taryn Barclay

Taryn Barclay is Corporate Responsibility Manager at IPC Media. Having previously worked in a Human Resources role for the BHP Billiton group in South Africa, Taryn joined IPC Media in 2002 as a HR Advisor. She was promoted to the newly created role of Corporate Responsibility Manager in April 2005 and in her current role, she is responsible for managing the company's community engagement activities, which includes the Charity of the Year programme, developing an environmental policy for the company, working with the brands to develop their own citizenship activities, and representing the company in key CSR forums in the UK.

Laura Baynham-Hughes

Laura Baynham-Hughes joined Help the Aged in June 2004 to manage the charity's strategic corporate partnerships, which include relationships with British Gas, Barclays and Zurich Community Trust. Laura is now heading up the 19-strong Corporate Fundraising and Events team at Help the Aged, which is responsible for managing a varied portfolio of corporate accounts and fundraising events. Prior to joining Help the Aged, Laura spent five years at the charity Action for Blind People working in both events and corporate fundraising, after studying Economics and Business at Newcastle University.

Susan Beck

Susan has been a professional fundraiser since 1997. She was formerly Corporate and Major Donor Fundraising Manager at The Romanian Orphanage Trust, now EveryChild. In 2000 Susan joined TreeHouse, the national charity for autism education, where she is Director of Fundraising. Susan holds an MSc in Charity Marketing and Fundraising. Her dissertation focused on pricing and evaluating Cause Related Marketing.

Catherine Bennett

Catherine Bennett (BA, MinstCert) is Head of Fundraising at FSID. She has spent nearly 10 years in Fundraising and has been a lead player in a host of successful corporate fundraising initiatives. Whilst at Breast Cancer Campaign she was instrumental in establishing a number of corporate partnerships leading to major and long term funding for the charity. In 2005 she led the Help the Aged Corporate Development team that secured the recently announced £1.4m strategic partnership with Barclays. During her time at FSID she has been responsible for focusing the strategy on areas with the most profitable potential and has developed a range of innovative Cause Related Marketing initiatives.

Laurie Boult

Laurie has worked in various marketing roles for eight years, specialising in cause related marketing at Breakthrough Breast Cancer for over five years. During this time Laurie has account directed several corporate partnerships including The Bingo Association, which she initially secured, and Marks & Spencer, which she took on in 2002 and grew from a Lingerie partnership to a cross business marketing campaign and Breakthrough's largest corporate partner. Both partnerships were award-winning in 2006 (Marks & Spencer taking the BITC CRM award and Breakthrough taking the Institute of Fundraising Most Effective Corporate Partnership Award for Bingo for Breakthrough). She currently manages an account management team, overseeing fourteen corporate partnerships. Business in the Community research has placed Breakthrough in the top three of all UK charitable causes and organisations benefiting from Cause Related Marketing programmes for the last four years.

Sara Bowcutt

Sara Bowcutt is Corporate Fundraising Manager at FSID. She has worked in Corporate Fundraising since 2003 and prior to that spent several years working in marketing in the commercial sector. Sara has been instrumental in delivering successful initiatives with businesses from a range of sectors from banking to FMCG to magazine publishing. Whether it be sponsorship, CRM or any other part of the corporate fundraising mix Sara's experience has given her a sound insight into what makes a corporate-charity tie up successful.

Alison Braybrooks

Alison Braybrooks has over 10 years experience in corporate/charity partnerships. After completing her business degree she worked in publishing and management consultancy. She then decided to focus her career in the voluntary sector. Her first role was with the Employers Forum on Disability, next as sponsorship manager for Macmillan Cancer Support, then heading up the corporate fundraising teams at NCH and Shelter. While working in the charity sector she was responsible for developing some significant long-term partnerships and guiding her teams to improve their new business and supporter management skills.

She is now at EDF Energy, running one of the most well-respected community programmes in the UK.

James Hayward

James Hayward currently works in corporate charity partnerships for BAE Systems helping to manage the corporate partnerships between charities and the employees. Most recently he has worked on partnerships with such organisations as The Stroke Association (2005/06) and Macmillan Cancer Support (2006 to date). In the past James has worked with ASDA and Anthony Worrall Thompson and a variety of other companies in cause related marketing projects. He also plays a mean blues guitar and is red belt in Traditional Kung Fu.

Joan Hemmery

Joan Hemmery is Head of Community Investment at HBOS. Her role involves managing the HBOS Foundation – a charity set up to support local communities throughout the UK.

Joan joined Bank of Scotland as a graduate trainee. Her early career was in the marketing area where she developed and established the youth sector for Bank of Scotland.

Joan is a member of The Marketing Society, the Institute of Direct Marketing, and a former Treasurer of Communicators in Business in Scotland.

Joan was educated at Cambridge House School, Ballymena and University of Stirling where she studied English and French.

Helen Hirons

Helen Hirons has worked as a fundraiser in the voluntary sector for 20 years. She has held posts at a number of charities including Barnado's and Breakthrough Breast Cancer where she pioneered the award winning fundraising campaign Fashion Targets Breast Cancer. Helen was also previously Head of Fundraising at Centrepoint.

Helen is currently Head of Corporate & Community Fundraising at Diabetes UK.

Josephine Job

Josephine Job MinstF(Cert) has worked in the Voluntary Sector for the Royal National Institute of the Blind since January, 2001, initially as a National Corporate Fundraiser and now managing the National Corporate Partnerships team which raises money from Companies across the UK.

Previous to working in the Voluntary sector Josephine managed the charity/community programme for ScottishPower and was responsible for implementing their PowerPartners Programme. She was also a member of the London Benchmarking Group and Community Practitioners Forum.

Josephine is an Executive Committee member of the Institute of Fundraising in Scotland and is an active member of the Institutes Income Generation Group.

Josephine lives in Scotland with her husband Charles and two dogs.

Robin Jones

Robin has worked in research and fundraising for 15 years, specialising in prospect research for the last10 years. In 2003, he set up his own business, Milestone Research (www.milestoneresearch.co.uk) where his clients include UK charities, cultural organisations and universities, as well European and US organisations.

Robin is an experienced trainer and has provided tailor-made courses for a number of clients. He has spoken on prospect research at many fundraising conferences organised by such bodies as the Institute of Fundraising, Directory of Social Change and, in the United States, APRA (Association of Professional Researchers for Advancement). He is currently chair of the Institute of Fundraising's special interest group, Researchers in Fundraising.

Mark Line

Mark Line is a pioneer of corporate social responsibility. He is the co-founder of csrnetwork – an international team of consultants that provides leading-edge services in benchmarking, performance management and report development. Mark works with large, multinational corporations in designing and implementing their CSR and sustainability strategies or on assurance assignments. His current clients include Airbus, Mittal Steel, StoraEnso and Vodafone.

Mark led a team that developed the indicator protocols for GRI's G3 and was part of a small team that advised GRI on assurance of its own first Sustainability Report.

He is also the co-founder of JustAssurance, whose assurance work for CFS was rated 1st in SustainAbility/Standard & Poors' last global benchmark of corporate sustainability reporting.

Mark jointly initiated the Accountability Rating ®, which ranks the world's largest companies, with leading institute, AccountAbility. The 2006 rating will be published in FORTUNE magazine in late October.

Ian MacQuillin

Ian MacQuillin is an account director at TurnerPR, a PR company that specialising in providing PR services to the fundraising sector. He was a journalist for 18 years and edited Professional Fundraising from 2001 to 2006. He has a geology degree and studied philosophy at the Open University.

Ita McMahon

Ita is the London Benchmarking Group adviser at The Corporate Citizenship Company. In her role, she develops tools and services to help members understand and apply the LBG model to their organisation. Ita also manages the LBG for Community Partners workshop programme.

Prior to joining The Corporate Citizenship Company, Ita was a policy adviser on emissions trading at the Department for Environment, Food and Rural Affairs. She has worked for Hitachi Europe Ltd, and as a co-ordinator of international relations for local government in Niigata, Japan.

Carla Miller

Carla has worked as a fundraiser for the past nine years at organisations including NSPCC and Action for Blind People in the UK and Ted Noffs Foundation in Australia. Her most recent roles include Head of Fundraising at Samaritans and Director of Fundraising and Marketing at Rainbow Trust Children's Charity.

Valerie Morton

Valerie Morton is a 'career' fundraiser, having joined the profession straight from University. She has held senior management roles in charities such as Help the Aged, NSPCC and RNIB.

Her extensive experience in corporate fundraising began at NSPCC where she was responsible for both the first one million pound company adoption of a charity with Asda and the development of a substantial stream of income from the then newly introduced payroll giving scheme.

In her current role as a fundraiser and consultant, Valerie has worked with many clients to develop innovative corporate partnerships and to maximise income from corporate relationships.

Valerie combines her role in the voluntary sector with being a Non Executive Director at East of England Strategic Health Authority and contributing to numerous voluntary Boards and Committees.

Beth Nicholls

Beth Nicholls manages United for UNICEF, the corporate partnership between UNICEF UK and Manchester United FC. Beth came to UNICEF from the sports industry, where she has worked closely with world class athletes and teams at numerous major international sporting events over the past decade including Summer and Winter Olympic Games, FIFA World Cup and World Games. Subsequently, Beth was responsible for UNICEF International's involvement in the 2004 Athens Olympic Youth Camp, and was then brought in by UNICEF UK to secure a third term for the United for UNICEF partnership and develop the strategy that would take the partnership to its tenth anniversary in 2009.

Andrew Peel

Andrew Peel is a freelance fundraising consultant. He has 14 years' experience of strategic corporate fundraising, having held senior positions at Sightsavers International, the British Red Cross, the Giving Campaign, Help the Aged and the Children's Society.

He has brokered, developed and managed a wide range of major corporate partnerships, including Help the Aged's adoption as Tesco Charity of the Year 1998 and more recently, Sightsavers' ground-breaking $6m international alliance with Standard Chartered Bank – the objective of which was one million sight restorations in three years. Andrew received the ICFM's Professional Fundraiser of the Year Award in 1997.

Anne-Marie Piper

Anne-Marie specialises in charity law and acts for sponsors of new charities, directors, trustees and officers of existing charities and other not-for-profit bodies and individuals and companies wishing to make charitable gifts or do business with charities. She is also well known for her handling of Charity Commission investigations and acting, for and against, Charity Commission appointed receivers and managers. Founder, former secretary and now Chairman of the Charity Law Association, Anne-Marie also lectures and writes regularly on charity law subjects.

Rachael Reeve

Rachael has worked in the retail sector for the past 11 years covering a variety of roles in both stores and central departments and has worked in the Marketing department at Marks and Spencer for the last seven years. As part of her role at Marks & Spencer Rachael leads the Lingerie Marketing Team and relationship with Breakthrough Breast Cancer, driving the CSR programme to deliver fundraising campaigns on an annual basis and new product opportunities within Lingerie in conjunction with Breakthrough Breast Cancer. Under Rachael's guidance the relationship with Breakthrough Breast Cancer has grown considerably from a once yearly fundraising focus in October for Breast Cancer Awareness Month to a year round integrated programme of marketing campaigns and new product launches resulting in delivery of annual fundraising targets in excess of £1.5m and the BITC Award for fundraising excellence in 2006.

Catherine Sermon

Catherine Sermon joined Business in the Community in 1998 after completing a Master of Arts in Marketing. Catherine has held a number of posts including campaigning, research and development and advisory services work on cause-related marketing, community investment and corporate social responsibility. In 2005, Catherine established the Business

Action on Health campaign, focused on embedding health into the corporate responsibility agenda with particular focus on engaging employers to improve the health and well-being of employees through the workplace. Currently Catherine is the Campaign Director for Cause Related Business, which aims to increase the positive impact of companies in the community, by promoting innovation and best practice.

Jill Taylor

Jill Taylor was Director of Fundraising and Communications at BIBIC – British Institute for Brain Injured Children – a national children's charity based in Somerset. During her five years in post the fundraising team expanded to include embracing a wider corporate remit, and income doubled. Jill believes the 'can-do' attitude of fundraisers is a vital commodity in gaining fundraising success to enable a charity of BIBIC's size to 'punch above it's weight' and encourages individuals to develop in their fundraising careers.

Jill was previously Chief Executive at a heritage charity and is currently Campaign Director for Exeter Cathedral's Third Millennium Appeal.

Philippa Thompson

Philippa has worked in the charity sector for over seven years at the RNLI in a variety of roles from London Marathon and Challenge events manager to Beach fundraising manager, responsible for the development of fundraising with RNLI Beach Lifeguards. Philippa now heads up the corporate fundraising team, working with key national corporate clients. Prior to this Philippa worked as an events manager and new business development manager looking after key clients and developing new business in event management agencies.

Michael Tuffrey

Mike is an executive director of The Corporate Citizenship Company and has worked in the field of corporate social responsibility since 1987. A chartered accountant by profession, Mike is founding editor of Corporate Citizenship Briefing, the leading journal for managers of social impact issues across the business. He founded The Corporate Citizenship Company with David Logan in 1997.

His career has encompassed being a director of a leading not-for-profit agency and working in Parliament as a researcher, speech writer and legislative assistant. His own voluntary activities include serving as national honorary treasurer of Gingerbread, the lone parent charity, and chairing the management committee of a care-in-the-community charity providing homes and work for people with a severe learning difficulty.

Foreword

There is much to interest and excite in this third edition of Corporate Fundraising. All the contributing authors are well respected practitioners who illustrate well the extent of good practice and innovation in the field of corporate fundraising today. Accurately reflected are the current climate of sophisticated competitive pitches; the need for community investment to impact on a company's bottom line; and increasing monitoring and evaluation of corporate partnerships.

An impressive array of case studies in part 2 of the book complements the nuts and bolts 'how to' explanations of part 1. There are case histories from both the charity and company perspective, giving valuable insights into the motivations and benefits behind partnerships from both sides. The Appendices of part 3 giving legal guidance, checklists and templates form a valuable resource.

It is refreshing to read success stories from charities such as TreeHouse and the Foundation for the Study of Infant Deaths proving that smaller charities can develop and manage successful corporate partnerships just as well as our household name voluntary organisations. Equally inspiring are long term relationships such as that between Marks and Spencer and Breakthrough Breast Cancer.

Experienced fundraisers will find the book a useful resource to dip into for reference and ideas, while those new to the profession will want to read it from cover to cover. Even hardened Chief Executives like me will find inspiration and innovation among its pages, and I suggest it is put on the mandatory reading list of corporate personnel planning or managing a charity partnership.

Melanie Burfitt
Chief Executive
Lymphoma Association

Introduction and acknowledgements

Collating complete information about how much charities receive in income as a result of corporate fundraising (CFR) is very difficult. Some statistics indicate that CFR accounts for as little as 4 per cent of total voluntary income to charities. If this is the case, why do charities, large and small, invest in this area of fundraising? After reading this book, the answer may become clearer.

First, companies can often leverage support in many forms, for example from their suppliers, staff and customers. Not all this income is captured in statistics which reflect actual corporate giving, and not income leverage though corporate influence. Income generated through the sale of pin badges is highly dependent upon the donating of space and access to company customers, and yet this income is rarely considered to be 'corporate'. CFR, when managed well, can contribute to the success of other areas of fundraising. After all, people do not compartmentalise or segment themselves in the way charities do their donors. A company CEO may also be a trustee of a grant-making trust and be a high net worth individual in their own right. Corporate partnerships can lead to significant non-financial benefits (or indirect financial benefits), such as awareness, membership generation and provision of expertise. Finally, since many employees who donate to charities through payroll giving are new donors to their chosen charity, how much of the £80 million-plus given in this way would never have found its way to charities without corporate involvement?

The outstanding success stories showcased in this third edition of *Corporate Fundraising* are testament to the valuable role this form of fundraising plays in the strategic mix for many charities.

I have included in this edition a full chapter detailing the history of corporate involvement in society. With so many people now joining the voluntary sector and seeing fundraising as a career, there is a danger that they will see history as beginning at the point they first become aware of it. As Chapter 1 shows, activities we may think of as current trends, such as sales promotions, were happening over 100 years ago. Before the dawning of the welfare state, companies' involvement in social issues was as great as it is now, even if the term 'corporate social responsibility' was not coined until many years later. Understanding the history and heritage of corporate community involvement is not only an essential for any corporate fundraiser but can also be a valuable source of ideas.

As corporate fundraisers, we all have a responsibility to follow best practice. This is summarised effectively in the Institute of Fundraising code of practice for charities working with business. The chapters in the first section of this book give each author's perspective on aspects of carrying out the corporate fundraising process.

What has been encouraging when sourcing examples of best practice and good case studies has been the excellent work being carried out by smaller charities. Reading about charities such as Foundation for the Study of Infant Deaths (Chapter 8), with an annual turnover of under £1.5 million, and their highly successful sales promotion through Grobag should be an inspiration to those charities which claim such promotions are for big brand name charities only.

The case studies from HBOS, BAE Systems and EDF Energy, for example, offer valuable insight into the mindset of the corporate sector. So often these days, as these examples demonstrate, charities are involved in some form of application or pitching process to become a chosen charity. Now that so many companies are running an 'adopted charity', and with the amounts at stake ranging from thousands to millions of pounds, charities are often faced with what can be called the 'lottery effect'. In reality, the chances of being selected to be the adopted charity can be quite low, but there is a temptation to apply for each available one, and to put substantial effort into trying to winning each one, because of the potential gain. There are learning points on both sides. Charities need to ensure they make strategic decisions about which partnership they should apply for and how much time to give to each one so that this aspect of new business is balanced with other prospective partnerships such as donations or cause-related marketing. Companies, for their part, need to be aware of the impact their 'carrot' of potentially large sums of money has on charities. It is not uncommon for charities to spend 20, even 50 or more person hours on an application and pitch, only to find that they are rejected for a reason which could have been identified at an early stage.

The fact that the companies showcased in this book have been happy to articulate their policies, procedures and practice is an indication of a move towards this greater transparency.

Acknowledgements

My sincere thanks go to all the chapter authors who have given so freely of their time and expertise. One of the most enjoyable aspects of working in the voluntary sector is the way people are happy to share their experiences with colleagues who may in some cases also be competitors. I am grateful to all the authors, from charities and companies, for their contributions which will benefit the sector as a whole.

Many other people have also been involved in supporting authors, so thanks also go to Adam Colling, Anne Euler, Ali Giles, Val Lord, Leo Visconti and Chris Baynham-Hughes, Rosemary Baronetti, Rachel Holmes and Kirstin Gaymer.

Finally, a personal thank you to my husband, Adrian Penrose, for introducing me to *Hart's Rules for Compositors and Readers* (compulsory reading for any editor) and to my son Leo Penrose for putting up with the injustice of being limited to one hour on the computer each day while his mother clearly exceeded this limit editing this book.

About this book

This book is in three parts. The first offers background and context to CFR, and sets out best practice in all aspects of managing and delivering CFR. The second part contains a wealth of case studies, from both corporate and charity perspectives. Part 3 – the Appendices – contains valuable factual information and templates which can be used for developing strategies and policies. Each chapter can be read individually and offers the personal viewpoint and experience of its author. Together, the chapters provide a full perspective of CFR.

Valerie Morton

PART 1
Background and best practice

CHAPTER ONE

The evolution of true corporate partnerships

Catherine Sermon

Today phrases such as cause-related marketing and corporate community investment are commonplace in the corporate fundraising world, and well known in many businesses. Understanding how they have developed, and why, sets us in good stead to view the corporate perspective for partnerships and to predict future developments.

The following account just scratches the surface of the extensive activity that shapes corporate and charity partnerships today, in order to demonstrate the thriving interdependence of the voluntary, corporate and public sectors.

Where did it all start?

The era of Victorian philanthropists is well documented. Many of the UK's most familiar companies and brands, such as Cadbury's, Unilever, Marks & Spencer, Boots and Sainsbury's, were founded on strong principles. These businesses were set up and run on an understanding of the clear economic and social benefits of their products and services. For example, Cadbury's was established on the basis that, by providing tea, coffee, cocoa and chocolate as an alternative to alcohol, it would help alleviate one of the primary causes of poverty and deprivation among working people at the time.

Although we often think of charity-related product promotions as being a recent invention, archives at the Royal National Lifeboat Institution document how Lever Brothers ran a competition on Sunlight soap as far back as 1887 to raise money to pay for a new lifeboat.

Such companies also put the well-being of their employees and their communities at the heart of how they did business. This included the introduction of benefits such as pensions and sickness payments for their employees long before government did so. It also involved consumer-facing campaigns such as that run in 1926 by Lever Brothers, who launched a Clean Hands campaign to encourage children to wash their hands by educating them about dirt and germs.

Social outreach extended well beyond their own consumers and employees. During the First World War, Cadbury's sent over 28,000 parcels of chocolate to servicemen. At this time they also demonstrated what must be one of the earliest examples of employee involvement, when they established two convalescent hospitals in Bournville, supported and run by Cadbury employees.

This involvement was replicated in the Second World War, when Cadbury kept Allied troops in chocolate and, despite rationing, sent out Mercy Vans with urns of hot cocoa during air raids. Similarly, during the 1941 Blitz, Unilever-owned Lifebuoy Soap provided a free emergency washing service via Lifebuoy vans equipped with hot showers, soap and towels, which visited bomb-struck areas of London.

For these companies, community involvement was not exclusive to times of emergency or even local communities. In these early years, recognising the importance of the supply chain, Cadbury set up social projects in Ghana including an agricultural training centre. Closer to home, in the 1930s Cadbury launched an activity-based scheme, 'Gifts for Scout Troops and Clubs', and in the 1950s they had a schools department, which offered visual aids for teachers and pupils.

Similarly, Sainsbury's has photographs of staff participation in local carnivals during the 1920s and 1930s and support for local charities was recorded in the *JS Journal* from the 1950s onwards. In 1965, the Sainsbury Charitable Fund was established to manage contributions to the voluntary sector, and by 1975 it employed full-time staff dedicated to managing charitable donations and community investment.

At the same time, the voluntary sector was developing further. Concepts that might seem to have the ring of the modern operating climate, such as promoting 'effective giving', were introduced. The Charities Aid Foundation, which was originally enshrined as the Charities Department of the National Council of Social Service (now the National Council for Voluntary Organisations) was set up with this aim in 1924, and in 1974 became independent charity we know today.

As the welfare state grew in power and reach, it changed the political and social backdrop that had prompted the early donors and war-time support. The pioneers upheld many of their founding principles and behaviours, but the post-war period did not herald significant growth in corporate community investment. Alongside a move towards public limited companies, new entrants to the market did not need, and were not expected, to involve themselves in social issues in the way of their predecessors, and often they did not.

The rise of corporate community investment

There is evidence of corporate charitable donations and cause-related marketing promotions during the 1950s, 1960s and 1970s, such as Heinz's association with NCH, the children's charity. Remarkably, Campbell Soup's 'Labels for Education' programme, which was introduced in the USA in 1973, continues today and is perhaps the longest-running example of cause-related marketing in the world. Corporate sponsorship of sporting and cultural events also emerged over this period, although most companies were neither particularly involved or integrated in their local communities.

Early 1980s

Significant attention did, however, turn to corporate community investment in the early 1980s. By this time the historic developments of the welfare state, such as pensions and the NHS, were firmly established, but stark gaps between the wealthiest and most disadvantaged remained, and in many places were widening. As a business response, in 1982, against a backdrop of high levels of unemployment and urban rioting, Business in the Community was established.

In 1984 the Industrial Committee for the NSPCC's centenary appeal helped the charity to achieve a significant milestone in corporate fundraising, contributing to the £15 million total raised. Critical to its success was that companies such as Laing, Trusthouse Forte and Habitat adopted the appeal via the involvement of their chairman or chief executive on the committee. While today companies tend to be more strategic or less autocratic about their charity selection criteria and process, the capacity of business leaders and a charity partnership to mobilise and engage employees and customers remains significant.

One leading company to respond to this changing context was Diageo (then Grand Metropolitan), which at this time had no formal community investment programme. However, the company's directors established a significant community programme to make a long-term impact on unemployment, particularly in the most disadvantaged areas of the UK, based on partnership with local communities and government agencies. To tackle this, Diageo set up Tomorrow's People Trust, and has invested over £25 million since then, in direct investment and through other forms of financial assistance.

The strength of the programme is to demonstrate two key aspects of corporate and charity cross-sector working. The first is to show clearly how companies can leverage further value beyond financial investment. The comprehensive support provided by Diageo has included access to business advice from Diageo's people on finance, corporate governance, communications, marketing, human resources, risk management, strategy and property. Employees have acted as mentors to clients of Tomorrow's People and Diageo-owned businesses have offered work placements, with over 500 employees actively involved to date. Tomorrow's People was also able to play a key role in helping individuals and communities when many of the old breweries closed.

The second key strength is the benefit of a true partnership approach for both organisations and wider society. For Diageo there have been business benefits in the form of employee skills development, enhanced reputation and positioning as a good corporate citizen. Tomorrow's People has helped over 380,000 people out of long-term unemployment, welfare dependency or homelessness, with over 150,000 being helped into work and three quarters going into and staying in full-time employment. Importantly, the experience of establishing and then working in close partnership acted as the catalyst for Diageo to develop a strategic global community investment programme in other markets around the world, supported by the Diageo Foundation.

It was also at this time that American Express was credited for coining the phrase 'cause-related marketing', although the concept had existed for many years. Its 1983 promotion tapped into the psyche of the American public by making a donation to the Statue of Liberty Restoration Fund for every new card enrolment and transaction during a promotional period. Its success put cause-related marketing firmly on the map in the USA and it is exciting therefore to see American Express, more than 20 years later, take a lead in promoting 'Red', raising money for the Global Aids Fund.

While both the American Express and Campbell Soup case studies demonstrate a cause-related marketing link to sales promotion, many early partnerships were formed around sponsorship. When Canon undertook sponsorship of the Football League in 1983, it was a relatively new brand in the UK, with marketing objectives to raise awareness. Canon identified the power of sport, and football in particular, to establish itself in the hearts and minds of UK consumers. High-profile sponsorship, which saw the Football League become the Canon League for three consecutive seasons, was a natural marketing platform.

How a company leverages a sponsorship, however, is often just as important as the association itself. To this end, Canon also sponsored youth football, encouraged players to act as inspiring role models in schools and youth clubs, and introduced awards which raised money for charities. These activities provided great platforms from which Canon could bring its sponsorship to life, and contributed towards the huge increase in brand awareness, from 18 to 80 per cent. Today many football clubs run powerful community programmes, some of which bring charities and the local community together with programmes involving their sponsors and fans.

Late 1980s

To both recognise achievement and encourage greater activity, in 1986 HRH the Prince of Wales launched the PerCent Club for Business in the Community, building on a concept he had seen in the USA a year earlier. At this time a small group of companies participated in capturing, calculating and reporting their community investment as a percentage of pre-tax profits. These companies bravely participated in that first year, when reporting publicly on community investment was a relatively new concept. Over the past 20 years, over 300 have now done so. Interestingly, it is not just large FTSE companies that use the PerCent model to capture and report their community investment, as many of the smaller companies allocate a far higher percentage.

Twenty years on, over £991 million-worth of cash, kind, time and other investment was reported by nearly 200 companies in 2006. Cash support continues to account for the majority of this contribution, but it includes over £91 million-worth of employee time dedicated to programmes. Encouragingly, this year, while the overall contribution made by participating companies increased, there was a reduction in the amount of this dedicated to management costs.

Also at this time, inspired by the approach of companies in the USA, which involved employees in both designing and delivering community investment, Whitbread set up what is widely credited as the first employee volunteering programme in the UK. An employee volunteer manager was appointed who, with the interest and support of colleagues, set up more than ten committees throughout the business within six months. Each committee was given £500 to donate in money or equipment to a community organisation and supported to do this in a range of different ways by the volunteer manager. At one stage over 50 committees throughout the UK were involved in a myriad of activities from fundraising and collecting books to reading in schools.

In 1989, a small group of professional firms came together driven by a recognition of the valuable role they could play in contributing to local community regeneration by giving services for free, not cash. Property firm Drivers Jonas was one of these and Christopher Jonas led the development of the Professional Firms Group, now known as ProHelp. Initially set up in London, it now has 35 local groups around the UK and approximately 1,000 professional firms involved.

While law firms, accountants, architects and surveyors make up the bulk of ProHelp membership, accounting for just over 61 per cent, other firms commit support from construction and engineering, management consultancy, property services, marketing, PR and design sectors. Relevant volunteering is at the centre of the value that businesses can utilise for charities and is relevant for more than just the professional firms. Boots No7 consultants use their time and expertise to support Look Good . . . Feel Better beauty workshops for women with cancer. Over 60 Boots people regularly volunteer by providing morale-boosting makeovers and advice on skin care and make-up in hospitals.

Early 1990s

By the early 1990s, when the UK was in recession, many companies had programmes of grants established, adopted charities of the year and were encouraging their employees to become involved in their local communities and raise money for charities. For example, Nestlé and WH Smith, as well as Whitbread, were actively celebrating employee community involvement, running Employee Volunteer and Community Service awards.

In 1992, Royal Mail set up its payroll giving scheme, which has become one of the most highly admired in the UK. Over 50,000 people, 30 per cent of its workforce, are actively donating to over 1,500 charities every month, and have donated over £30 million. Royal Mail also demonstrates how maximum effect can be generated by integrating the different aspects of employee fundraising. Since selecting Help the Hospices as its charity of the year, 14,000 employees have chosen to support the charity through payroll giving.

One of the strongest examples of cause-related marketing continues to be the Avon Breast Cancer Crusade, also launched in 1992, as the company was moved by the scale and impact of breast cancer on women's and therefore on their customers, employees and their families' lives. In its first year Avon raised £1 million for Breakthrough Breast Cancer in the UK. Since then, they have raised over $400 million from campaigns run in 50 different countries. Over time, by having this umbrella cause they have been able to export it, tailor it and work with different charities. In the UK they have raised over £12 million and worked with Breakthrough Breast Cancer, Breast Cancer Care and Macmillan Cancer Support. Cause-related marketing has made a valuable contribution to charities beyond the direct benefits that include raised awareness and fundraising. It has provided a commercial win–win business case for working in partnership with the private sector.

Research conducted by Business in the Community at this time, among over 80 charities, identified a swing, however, towards project funding and away from core funding. This shift was largely driven by companies wishing to focus their attention and support on specific and relevant aspects of a charity's work, as they started to align their support to their business strategy. This remains a sticking point for the voluntary sector, as it marked a shift away from unrestricted funds, which are vital to cover the core operational costs a charity needs just to exist.

By 1994, many companies were taking a structured approach to corporate community investment including;

- reflecting management structure and culture in the management of corporate community investment and setting objectives

- clearly defining the role of a central function and operating units

- coordinating all activity, including charitable trusts

- supporting in the form of cash, staff time and gifts in kind

- developing formal policies.

A focus on measurement and benchmarking is demonstrative in any environment that something is being taken more seriously. Credit is due, therefore, to the six founding members of the London Benchmarking Group (LBG), which was set up in 1994 to develop and test a model for measuring their corporate community investment. This work involving BP, Diageo, IBM, Marks & Spencer, NatWest Group and Whitbread, led to the publication of basic principles and the LBG model in 1997. More detailed information about LBG can be found in Chapter 6.

Late 1990s

The donation of gifts in kind to charities is another vehicle for corporate investment beyond financial resource and employee volunteering. When In-Kind Direct (then called Gifts in Kind UK) was first constituted as a charity in 1996, on the initiative of HRH the Prince of Wales, it was the first charity in the UK to broker the donation of gifts of products and equipment from businesses to the voluntary sector. In 1997 it launched its first catalogue, two pages long with ten items. This has expanded dramatically and, constantly adapting to new technology, the charity's last catalogue carried over 600 lines, from toiletries to toys. In 10 years over 3,800 charities have benefited from this service, while companies have been able to save the costs and environmental impact associated with landfill.

Understanding the value of supporting the infrastructure for delivery as well as making gifts in kind, in 1997 Sainsbury's seconded an employee to work inside the charity FareShare. FareShare works to relieve food poverty by providing food and support to organisations working with homeless and disadvantaged people. Initially, the secondee helped ensure that FareShare had efficient logistics and satisfactory standards. However, the secondment was extended for a further two years to develop a national network of FareShare projects. At the same time, Sainsbury's made a financial contribution, which enabled the charity to leverage matched funding from the Lottery. For the company, FareShare is now an able and trusted partner to redistribute surplus foods in a safe and practical way.

Where did this lead us?

Some of the companies whose examples shaped much of what happens today continue to lead and innovate. This shows that, when community investment is embedded into the culture of an organisation, it is a sustainable investment. For example, Marks & Spencer's partnership with Breakthrough Breast Cancer has evolved over the years from fundraising to a more holistic partnership. Their launch in 2006 of the first ever high-street lingerie range for women who have undergone breast cancer surgery is a testament to the value and expertise of the charity sector to businesses.

Throughout this history a shift towards businesses providing in-kind support has been identified, but while this support is valuable, it cannot fully replace charities' need for income. In achieving a balance, Barclay's new partnership with Leonard Cheshire is a good example where business expertise is put to relevant use for the charity's core aims, alongside a financial investment to underpin this work. So while both organisations are working towards their shared aim of supporting over 600 disabled people to establish their own business, and Barclays employees will act as mentors, the charity's ability to deliver is backed by a total investment from Barclays of over £2.5 million over three years.

Donor or partner

The charities that are now the most successful are those that secure long-term business partners and share with them their organisational purpose and strategy. By doing this they are able to engage companies in support for the organisation generally as well as for specific projects.

The balance of power between charities and companies is also often discussed. It is encouraging that there is an increasing number of partnerships in which charities feel on equal footing with their corporate partners, but it would be misleading to think that this is always the case. Stories of last-minute cancelled meetings, closed doors to senior employees and decision makers, and a lack of respect unfortunately remain too commonplace in the modern fundraising environment.

The growth of corporate fundraising, partnership and engagement teams however has enabled many charities to be clear on their proposition, the expertise that they offer and the value of this both to the cause they represent and the company they are working with. Charities such as the British Heart Foundation have clear criteria for companies they will work with and will not work in partnership with those that do not meet them, particularly for high-profile activities such as cause-related marketing.

Conclusion

Community investment is common in most large companies. Smaller organisations are involved, though more often than not without the terminology or acronyms. Corporate and charity partnerships old and new continue. In the UK, however, many feel that the mainstreaming of community investment has slowed innovation. Companies and charities must look for different ways of working together and break new ground.

Some of the most innovative developments are often those that provide a fresh approach or new model for partnership working. A new charity, v, was created following a government review into youth action and engagement. It now aims to attract 1 million new youth volunteers, aged 16–25, by 2010. As an independent charity supported by government funding, v is able to encourage companies, individuals, trusts and charities to work together with the lure of matched funding of their investment, whether that be in cash or kind.

As the demands on large companies increase, it would be all too easy to cut the time and budgets dedicated to the traditional community investment dimension of corporate responsibility. This could result in time-pressed business managers turning their attention to other aspects of the responsible business agenda with which they are less familiar. The voluntary sector must continue, therefore, to be clear on the shared benefits of corporate partnerships, and it must do more to understand the business environment, so as to be able to work effectively, without ever compromising or straying too far from its core purpose.

The community is at the heart of all corporate responsibility. It is where people, customers and employees live and work, whether referring to vulnerable customers and social exclusion, to education, skills and employability for the workforce, or the environment. Those companies and charities that recognise the strategic importance of understanding the community – and not just the pigeon-holing or traditional role of community investment – will be those that are attractive partners to the voluntary sector and will thrive in the future.

CHAPTER TWO

What is corporate social responsibility?

Mark Line

There is increasing pressure today on companies not just to share their wealth with society through sponsorship and donations but also to demonstrate that their core business activities are at best a benefit to society and at worst pose no threat. At the heart of the corporate–charity relationship is the issue of corporate social responsibility (CSR).

Essentially, CSR means understanding and managing a company's impacts on the broader economy, the environment and society. These impacts are potentially wide ranging and can include everything from labour standards in the supply chain, through environmental quality around a factory site, to the way in which economic benefits are shared with those affected by a company's operations. Understanding the expectations of a company's stakeholders – for example its clients, suppliers, employees, funding organisations, advocacy groups, and communities – provides the bedrock for understanding these CSR risks and opportunities.

Their expectations can extend well beyond simply 'what is required' by legislation as some stakeholders want to see that a company is transparent in the way it communicates its wider performance and that it behaves ethically and is well managed with strong governance processes. They not only want a company to be responsible in its actions, attitudes and values and able to be trusted but also expect it to be responsive to their needs and views.

For a company to take account of its impacts on society and the environment, it must first understand what these impacts might be. To be complete, its appreciation of these issues needs to include a suitable form of engagement with its stakeholders. Through effective engagement – and transparency over the results – a company can build a relationship with the world outside and – of equal importance – within the organisation, by understanding and managing its employees' expectations and demands.

The history of CSR

Financial success through delivery of sustainable profit and financial capital growth has been the traditional measure of a company's level of success. The way in which that profit is created however, raises significant questions over a company's social, environmental and broader economic performance, which have, in part, led to the concept of CSR.

In the 1970s the environmental movement emerged in response to concerns over resource depletion and pollution, leading to increasing regulation. By the 1980s, some large companies were beginning to think strategically about the environmental impact of their business and had developed environmental reporting and management systems. This practice of corporate environmental reporting acted as an 'ice breaker' for much wider formats for reporting on social and environmental issues.

However, not all companies responded and a number of high-profile scandals kept business practice under the microscope.

Union Carbide, a US chemical company, experienced one of the first major environmental and human safety disasters involving both employees and local communities at its pesticide plant in Bhopal, northern India. In 1984 the plant leaked 40 tonnes of toxic gases, killing between 2,000 and 8,000 people. The accident sparked a vigorous debate about company standards, and the variance between the levels of attention paid to the environment and safety in developing countries as compared to their practices at home. Other disasters followed – such as Chernobyl and the Exxon Valdez oil spill – and public confidence in the ability of big business to act responsibly plummeted.

Shell International rose to the forefront of public attention in 1994 over its involvement in Nigeria. Just a year later it was under scrutiny again when it tried to dump the Brent Spar platform in the North Sea. The public outcry and criticism these events received had not been experienced by a leading multinational corporation before, and they raised questions over the responsibility not just of Shell, but all multinationals.

Public outcry resulted in the emergence of more legislation and standards to drive better practice. The scope of new legislation went beyond enforcement of technical environmental standards and started to address the way in which the companies themselves were run. The collapse of Enron and Worldcom, for example, led to the introduction of the Sarbanes–Oxley act in the USA requiring widespread change to company internal controls and reporting.

Despite these changes, more corporate scandals followed, like the downfall of Italian food giant Parmalat, Shell's overestimation of its oil reserves, the collapse of Farepak in the UK and significant operational problems with BP's operations in the USA. These events continue to fuel pressure from both the general public and, increasingly, from shareholders for companies to reflect upon their responsibilities and how they should be managed.

One significant element of the business response to these developments has been the rise of corporate reporting to demonstrate greater transparency. Ever since the publication of the first environmental accounts, corporate responsibility (CR) reporting has risen steadily and substantially in the past three years. In 2005, 52 per cent of G250 companies issued separate CR reports, compared with 45 per cent in 2002.[1] In 2004, the UK government announced new legislation requiring large UK-quoted companies to produce an operating and financial review (OFR). Originally, this was intended to supplement existing reporting requirements by providing improved qualitative, non-financial and forward-looking information on the performance of the company. Although the final legislation adopted in 2006 was softened, it introduced the requirement for companies to publish a business review, mirroring a trend internationally towards greater mandatory disclosure on social and environmental impacts.

During this period, the finance sector has transformed its attitude towards CSR, which is significant given the sector's influence on who has access to capital. Research undertaken by csrnetwork has revealed a significant improvement in the accountability of global financial sector companies. In 2004 the average finance sector score in the Accountability Rating™, a measure of a company's engagement with the CSR agenda, was 18 per cent; this rose to 30 per cent in 2006.[2] There has been a significant and continuing rise in socially responsible or ethical investment (SRI) which generally either favours less 'damaging' companies or seeks to actively engage to influence investee company behaviour. According to Eurosif, the European Social Investment Forum, in 2006 the European SRI market was valued at over €1 trillion.

Some recent initiatives

There has been a significant effort to develop suitable tools and standards to support businesses in their CSR. Many of these have been developed by independent organisations and international fora set up specifically for that purpose; others have been put together by companies that are trying to determine what CSR means for them.

In the 1990s, management systems and reporting indicators for environmental stewardship led the way. The ISO 14000 series, for example, has

---

1 Source: *KPMG International Survey of Corporate Responsibility Reporting*, KPMG, 2005.
2 Source: www.accountabilityrating.com

become a widely adopted set of standards and guidelines which are widely recognised and generally respected as a set of environmental management tools – although some have criticised the standards' emphasis on technical expertise at the expense of wider stakeholder inputs.

More recently, even though many different approaches and guidelines exist, the concept of a 'global architecture of standards' is emerging and a convergence of standards is expected. In 2006, for example, the Global Reporting Initiative (see below) signed an agreement with the Global Compact, representing a significant alliance between organisations focused on disclosures and principles. It is likely that this process of mutual recognition and convergence will continue.

Below are highlighted the more established or influential initiatives.

OECD Declaration

As early as 1976, the member governments of the Organisation for Economic Co-operation and Development (OECD) adopted the OECD Declaration on International Investment and Multinational Enterprises, one part of which is the Guidelines for Multinational Enterprises. The guidelines are recommendations promoted by the 30 member governments for multinational enterprises (MNEs) operating in or from their country. The unique characteristic of these guidelines is that they are the only comprehensive, multilaterally endorsed code of conduct for MNEs in the world. The voluntary guidelines seek to encourage better understanding and co-operation between MNEs and the countries in which they operate. To this end, they are supported and at times revised by business and labour organisations, non-governmental organisations and the member governments.

The United Nations Global Compact

In 2000, the United Nations launched its Global Compact, which was drawn up in response to a challenge to world business leaders by UN Secretary General Kofi Annan to help build a more sustainable global economy that benefits all the world's people. The UN Global Compact is a set of ten principles based on existing international conventions such as the Universal Declaration of Human Rights, the International Labour Organisation's (ILO) Fundamental Principles on Rights at Work, the Rio Principles on Environment and Development and the UN Convention against Corruption. The principles cover the four areas of human rights, labour, environment and corruption.

Through the power of collective action, the Global Compact seeks to promote responsible corporate citizenship so that business can be part of the solution to the challenges of globalisation. It is not a regulatory instrument – it does not 'police', enforce or measure the behaviour or actions of companies. Rather, the Global Compact relies on public account-ability, transparency and the enlightened self-interest of companies, labour and civil society to initiate and share substantive action in pursuing the principles upon which the Global Compact is based. Signatories are, however, expected to produce an annual report on progress towards the compact's principles (which explains the reasoning behind an alliance with the Global Reporting Initiative, GRI). In contrast to the OECD MNE guidelines, the UN Global Compact seeks to involve all the relevant social actors: governments, which defined the principles on which the initiative is based; companies, whose actions it seeks to influence; labour, in whose hands the concrete process of global production takes place; civil society organisations, representing the wider community of stakeholders; and the United Nations, the world's only truly global political forum, as an authoritative convener and facilitator.[3] Since its official launch in 2000, the initiative had grown by 2006 to involve nearly 3,000 participants, including over 2,500 businesses in 90 countries around the world which are imple-menting the ten principles.

ISO 26000

A new voluntary Guideline Standard for Social Responsibility planned for publication in 2008 is ISO 26000, developed to be consistent with other existing ISO standards. Unlike ISO 14000, however, the 26000 series is not expected to include a certifiable management system standard, mirroring ISO 14001. Rather, the intention is to offer broad-ranging guidance for those organisations addressing their social responsibilities. ISO 26000 will emphasise performance results and improvements. Although the ultimate decision-making processes for ISO standards are limited to national stan-dards bodies, which is a significant limitation in terms of accountability, there is multi-stakeholder involvement during the development process and there has been a significant involvement from less developed countries which should help to build legitimacy for the new guidelines.

AA 1000

Transparency, accountability and stakeholder engagement are the buzz words that describe the key components of any CSR strategy. The leading London-based think tank, AccountAbility developed its AA 1000 frame-work to formalise these concepts and turn them into processes that can

---

3 Source: www.unglobalcompact.org

become practical tools for CSR management. AA 1000 is therefore a framework standard which is applicable to organisations in any sector of any size and in any region, which focuses particularly on transparency through ethical accounting, auditing and reporting. It is comprised of the AA 1000 Purpose and Principles, a Framework for Integration, an Assurance Standard and a Stakeholder Engagement Standard, although new modules and elements continue to be added.[4]

SA 8000

SA 8000 is a set of social accountability standards against which companies can be audited. The standard covers issues such as child labour, forced labour, health and safety, freedom of association, and discrimination, and has been widely used by companies with operations or suppliers in countries where these issues are especially relevant. Achieving certification against the standard is seen by many as a useful means of displaying their commitment to social accountability and CSR.

The Global Reporting Initiative

The GRI Sustainability Reporting Guidelines were developed by the Global Reporting Initiative,[5] a multi-stakeholder process involving representatives from diverse voices including business sector, environmental and human rights groups. The guidelines are a framework for combined economic, environmental and social reporting. They provide a widely accepted and popular voluntary framework for sustainability reporting. The framework includes a set of principles for reporting, metrics (indicators) intended to be applicable to all business enterprises and also sector-specific metrics, and a uniform format for reporting information integral to a company's sustainability performance.

The popularity of the GRI is mainly due to the clear direction provided on report content including the definition of a set of performance indicators. The GRI is not a prescriptive 'recipe' for the structure of a report, so reporting companies have been able to reflect the common elements as set out in the guidelines, without losing the necessary individuality and focus of their reports. The guidelines are now seen by many as an effective mechanism for achieving the transparency required by stakeholders.

The first draft guidelines of the GRI were released in 1999. Based upon the initial feedback, these were followed by the 2002 Sustainability

---

4 Source: www.accountability21.net
5 Source: www.globalreporting.org

Reporting Guidelines. The new, third revised or G3 version of the GRI framework was launched in October 2006 after a substantial process of consultation and user feedback. Although it is accepted that the guidance will continue to evolve, G3 represents a significant milestone in the mission to develop a uniform approach to sustainability reporting.

The question of exactly 'what to report?' remains a dilemma for many companies. At the extreme, some would say that the stakeholders of a company should have a strong influence on what should be reported. However, each stakeholder group will have different priorities, and mapping these out can be an exercise which in itself can yield valuable intelligence about how the company is perceived. As reports grow in size and complexity, there has been a growing recognition that they should focus on what is most important to have the greatest impact. This concept has been termed 'materiality'. AccountAbility has published significant practitioner-based guidance to support the Relevance and Materiality GRI principle.

GRI is fast becoming the global de facto standard in sustainability reporting. Since its inception in 1997, nearly 1,000 organisations have referenced the GRI guidelines in their sustainability reports.

Benchmarking

The use of benchmarking tools offers one way in which corporations can be held to account in terms of their environmental and social responsibility. The ability to compare the relative position of companies within and across sectors has become a significant driving force in the evolving CSR agenda.

A number of different ratings, rankings and benchmark surveys are currently available. Some evaluate the quality of non-financial reporting while others take into account company performance and underlying systems. The Accountability Rating™ draws on the AA 1000 series and assesses the systems a company has in place as it is believed that if a company has the right governance structures and management systems in place it will be able to derive good performance from these systems. The Rating is applied to the largest global companies and also at a country level and is revealing significant variances and a catalogue of best practice which companies that are relatively new to the agenda can draw upon.

The fundraising context

It is in this context of increasing environmental and social accountability that corporate fundraising now has to take place. Today fundraisers and donors are looking for a working partnership that provides mutual benefit not only in terms of funds but also, and often equally importantly, in terms of publicity and reputation. Companies and charities alike are careful

Accountability Rating™ criteria

Domain	Key features sought
Stakeholder engagement (20%)	• Identification of stakeholders, systematic engagement with them and assessment of their views on non-financial (economic, social and environmental) impacts that are material • Demonstration that the company has understood their views and responded to them • Institutionalisation of stakeholders into the company's decision-making processes
Governance (15%)	• Integration of non-financial issues and performance into Board level decision-making • Clear allocation of responsibilities for non-financial matters • Comprehensive global company policies on non-financial issues • Integration of non-financial performance into annual reporting
Strategy (20%)	• Alignment of core business strategy to the imperatives of sustainable development, and commitment to key voluntary frameworks and standards • Clear identification of non-financial impacts arising from the company's core operations • Influence of non-financial impacts on strategic business decisions
Performance Management (15%)	• Clear lines of management responsibility • Incentives and training to drive performance on non-financial issues • Management systems for non-financial issues, and product and process innovation to improve non-financial performance
Assurance (15%)	• Company's current and future assurance position on non-financial aspects of performance • Scope of assurance of the company's non-financial performance data by an independent third party • Materiality and completeness of the data reported, and responsiveness of the company to stakeholder concerns • Statement of the assuror's independence and competencies
Public Disclosure	• Alignment of non-financial reports with the GRI sustainability reporting guidelines • Material information published on the company's non-financial performance within its reporting

to choose fundraising partners that are likely to reflect well on their own operations. Fundraising is not about raising funds in whatever way possible; it is about using the partnership to develop a common approach.

For charities this means ensuring that their corporate partner is doing the right thing in terms of CSR and that they are not at risk of becoming embroiled in scandal and misconduct. In addition, charities need to be clear on their brand values and worth in any relationship with a corporate.

For the company, one aspect of corporate giving is selecting causes that fulfil the company policies on CSR or sustainable development and promote the industry sector in which they operate. Here it is crucial that the company policies on CSR also align with the core business strategy of the company in order to be perceived by external stakeholders as honest involvement in a worthy cause.

A large number of companies now have their own charitable foundations registered as charities from which they conduct their social investment programmes, donating both time and funds. In most cases the work of the foundation complements the attitudes and policies of the parent company. One of the programmes of the Shell Foundation, which was established in 1999, is the Sustainable Energy Programme. SEP supports not-for-profit projects all over the world that are developing and researching sustainable energy solutions and consumption.

As well as choosing causes that complement and further their business activities, companies use charities in cause-related marketing. This marketing may be defined as a commercial activity by which businesses and charities or causes form a partnership with each other for mutual benefit.[6] It is suggested that the quality of this partnership can be enhanced when there is some linkage in terms of product focus, the cause and the company's values as well as a product link. Research by Business in the Community has found that consumers increasingly expect companies to involve themselves in the local community: 81 per cent of consumers agree that they are more likely to buy a product or service that is associated with a cause they care about, price and quality being equal; 75 per cent of chief executives, marketing directors and community affairs directors believe that cause-related marketing can enhance corporate or brand reputation.

In a world where consumers and stakeholders are making ever more vociferous demands of today's business community, companies are having to reassess not only their involvement in the local community but also the core values that drive their business. Charities are keen to team up, but not at any price.

6 Source: Business in the Community, www.bitc.org.uk

CHAPTER THREE

How companies support charities

Laura Baynham-Hughes

Charities can receive support from companies and their employees in a variety of ways. The mechanisms used will often depend upon the company the charity is looking to work with and the relationship the charity currently has with them. This chapter outlines the main mechanisms at a charity's disposal and some of the key aspects of best practice to help maximise income from each source.

Community investment

Community investment involves the provision of financial support to community projects. The funding is often directed through charities and is one of the most traditional forms of corporate fundraising. This type of support may be considered philanthropic, whereby a donation is given to a charity and benefits are measured in terms of project outcomes rather than benefits to the company. Companies that give in this way often look to support charities that are local to them or ones that work for a cause area they, and their staff, feel strongly about.

Over recent years the corporate sector has started to take a more strategic approach to community investment by choosing themes and areas connected with their business. The strategic partnership approach is mainly adopted by larger companies, especially those in the FTSE 100. By choosing to support an area that is aligned to their core business, companies can add value to their investment. Not only can they give financial support but they can also potentially use their expertise, supply chains, employees, partners and customers to maximise the impact on the community. Examples of strategic partnerships are banks investing in financial literacy programmes, such as Barclays' recently launched three-year money management programme with Help the Aged and NCH, and mobile phone companies investing in disability charities, such as Vodafone's partnership with the National Autistic Society. This approach fits with the current CSR agenda (see Chapter 2).

Managing the programme

It is imperative that the charity is confident it can deliver the programme effectively and achieve the objectives set out at the start of the relationship. Thorough and detailed planning before embarking on the partnership is a key to success, as is jointly setting clear targets and objectives. Balancing the inputs to the programme (such as money, time and other resources) against the outputs and the impact they are aiming to deliver for the beneficiaries, the community and the corporate partner enables clear understanding and a strong business case for all parties. The result is a clear, focused programme and expectations are managed from the outset.

As the programme progresses, the main role for the corporate fundraiser is to ensure the charity is delivering on the agreed targets. Working closely with colleagues in programme delivery and other teams such as PR is essential. Setting up a steering group which meets regularly can aid communication internally and provide the corporate fundraiser with a mechanism to ensure the programme is on track and hitting targets, as well as identifying any issues and risks. Systems and procedures should be set up internally to provide the information required for the charity to monitor performance and report back to the corporate partner. Effective stakeholder management is a key success factor. Clear, comprehensive reporting to agreed timescales ensures the corporate partner is informed of progress against the objectives, thus enabling them to manage their stakeholders and to embed the programme into their business. This ongoing evaluation is critical. More information on evaluation is provided in Chapter 9.

Employee fundraising

Employee fundraising can be an informal arrangement driven by one or a few enthusiastic employees who encourage their colleagues to join them in fundraising for a particular charity or cause. Alternatively it can be a more formal arrangement whereby the company chooses to support an adopted charity for a specific period of time. This is communicated to staff and they are supported and encouraged to get involved. Traditionally charities have been adopted for a year, but increasingly companies are adopting charities for longer time periods.

Employee fundraising can deliver benefits for all key stakeholders. It has the potential to raise significant income for the charity, with large charity of the year adoptions raising upwards of £100,000 and leading partnerships raising in excess of £1 million. A relationship of this kind will involve interaction between many areas of the charity and company, helping to build a strong and hopefully lasting relationship. Direct communication with employees provides an excellent opportunity to raise awareness of the charity and build long-term loyalty and support. If the company offers payroll giving (see page 27) there is also the potential to secure a regular income stream for the charity which lasts beyond the adopted period.

Employee fundraising can also generate positive media coverage for both organisations. The company builds its brand and reputation among staff, customers and the wider community, as well as potentially gaining more tangible business benefits, such as increased footfall in stores. The charity increases awareness in the local community and positions itself as a valuable partner for the corporate sector.

Increasingly, companies are looking to their community programmes to provide development opportunities for their employees. Fundraising events and activities can improve team-building and communications skills, as well as increasing staff morale and motivation.

There are some potential drawbacks of this type of corporate fundraising. Securing, planning and managing employee fundraising initiatives can be time-consuming for a charity and the amount of money raised may not justify the time invested. These initiatives can also require up-front investment in resources such as fundraising materials (posters, collection boxes, fundraising packs). There is also a risk to the charity's reputation if the initiative fails. If the charity does not deliver or the company's expectations are unrealistic, this can reflect badly on the charity and the company may not subsequently be willing to provide a positive recommendation.

The adoption process – key issues

Identify target companies

Research and identify which companies adopt a charity of the year. Applying for charity of the year partnerships can be a resource-intensive process, so it is important to calculate your chance of success and be strategic in whom you target. Your charity may have a compelling offering which is easy to communicate which would really appeal to staff, so why not focus on partnerships decided by employees. Alternatively your charity's proposition may not be easily understood, but you can demonstrate that you can deliver business benefits to a company. So partnerships which are decided by the CEO may provide you with the best opportunity for success.

Ensure you can deliver

It is imperative that you clearly assess whether the charity has the resources, infrastructure and willingness internally to deliver, if you are successfully adopted. A number of large charity of the year partnerships are with retail chains that span the country and are often worth in excess of £1 million. The rewards are high; however, so are the expectations from the company and significant resources are needed to manage these partnerships effectively. There is a high risk involved to the charity's reputation if you were to proceed without the capacity to meet the company's requirements.

Match your approach to the process

Companies choose who they support in a variety of ways. The decision can be made by a committee or individual, or staff and customers may have the ultimate say. The proposal and approach should be tailored to reflect the process, the audience and the criteria the company has set. It can be beneficial to talk to the current and past charities that the company has supported to find out how the process worked for them, whether they have any advice and how they have benefited from the partnership.

Making the partnership a success

A successful employee fundraising partnership needs the company to be committed to the initiative with buy-in from the top. If staff around the company see senior employees at the company engaged and involved, this will encourage and motivate them to get involved too.

Setting and agreeing clear targets and objectives from the outset is recommended, as is developing a plan for the fundraising period. The plan should outline a calendar of activities, areas of responsibility, deadlines and resources committed on both sides. When setting targets, key areas for consideration are income generation, numbers of staff involved, media coverage generated, volunteering hours, gifts in kind, etc.

Where possible, put a contract in place outlining what has been agreed. Some companies may not wish to draw up a formal contract. However, if the charity is committing investment up front on the promise of income at a later date, it must take a formal decision whether to proceed at risk or not. A company cannot commit their staff to raise money, so the contract can only cover specifics such as corporate donations. In some cases the company may be willing to underwrite employees' fundraising efforts, guaranteeing a minimum sum.

If a contract is not put in place, the charity can produce minutes of meetings and ask for the company's written agreement that they provide an accurate record of what has been discussed and agreed. This is critical since any unexpected change in personnel on either side of the relationship could lead to a disagreement and unwanted consequences.

The charity must deliver its promises for the initiative to be successful. For example, if a dedicated account manager or PR support has been promised, it is essential that they are put in place in accordance with the agreement. Nominating key contacts at both organisations is essential for a smooth-running partnership. Setting up a steering group with representation from all key stakeholders which meets regularly is also recommended. This group should be responsible for monitoring and reviewing progress against targets and objectives.

The partnership may benefit from the company appointing a dedicated member of staff to manage the initiative. Experience has shown that encouraging staff from around the business to be 'charity champions' is a key driver of success. Companies that do not have this structure in place should be encouraged to follow this model. Communicating with key stakeholders about how they can get involved and the successes of the partnership will increase involvement and ultimately the income generated. Incentives for staff, such as a prize for the top fundraiser, can also help maximise income.

The ultimate success factor is to manage the partnership so effectively that the company decides to extend the partnership and support the charity for a further year.

Cause-related marketing

Business in the Community (BiTC) defines cause-related marketing (CRM) as 'a commercial activity by which businesses and charities or causes form a partnership with each other to market an image, product or service for mutual benefit'.

By taking a more commercial approach, CRM enables charities to access marketing and commercial budgets within companies, thereby widening the potential pool of investment. However, this does mean that charities have greater competition than they would for charitable donations, as they are also competing against advertising and PR agencies. Charities must be professional and commercially minded to compete for these resources and win.

There are no robust figures on the exact level of spend on CRM activity by UK companies. However, BiTC's Cause Related Marketing Tracker 2004 found that over £51.4 million was raised for charities and good causes through 66 CRM programmes during 2004. Other research from BiTC shows that 48 per cent of consumers said that cause-related marketing motivated them to switch brand, increase usage or try a new product, and 70 per cent of consumers reported a positive impact on behaviour or perception after exposure to a CRM programme.

Mutual benefit

A successful partnership is one that benefits both parties. Examples of successful CRM partnerships range from Tesco's sponsorship of Cancer Research's Race for Life events to Persil's on-pack promotions for Comic Relief.

Potential benefits of CRM to the company:

- raises awareness of the company, brand or product
- enhances the reputation of the above
- increases sales
- attracts and retains customers, increasing loyalty
- motivates employees
- provides differentiation in the marketplace
- benefits the community in which the company operates.

Potential benefits of CRM to the charity:

- increases income
- raises awareness of the cause/issue
- broadens the fundraising portfolio
- enhances both reputation and brand
- offers the opportunity to develop new partnerships
- provides new channels of communication.

There are a few issues to bear in mind when embarking on a CRM partnership. First, the long-term potential can be limited since many corporate marketers are typically in their roles for a short time and are seeking a quick win before they move on. Another danger to watch out for is a company using a charity or good cause cynically to divert attention from or clean up their reputation following a transgression. Research is therefore key before embarking on a relationship of this nature.

Bear in mind the balance of power between charity and company. In theory this should be equal; in reality it is often biased in favour of the company, as the organisation that holds the pursestrings may be perceived to be in charge. Charities can try to avoid this by having a thorough and accurate understanding of the value of their assets, which will enable them to negotiate with confidence. Charities may consider guidance from an external expert to help with valuation.

Keys to CRM success

BiTC outlines six key elements to a successful CRM partnership.

1 Planning and preparation – Research into potential partners is key to ensuring a clear fit. Partners must define and agree the scope of the partnership and secure commitment from both parties.

2 Negotiating the partnership – Align objectives, audit assets, define the activity, value the opportunity and assess the risks.

3 The formal agreement – It is vital that a formal agreement is put in place, covering legal requirements, responsibilities and liabilities. For more information on the need for robust contracts and the legal requirements surrounding partnerships of this kind see Appendix One page 153.

4 Managing the programme – Set out clear responsibilities, timelines, objectives and monitor performance.

5 Communicating the programme – Communicate effectively internally and externally.

6 Monitor, measure and evaluate the programme.

By following these principles, charities and their corporate partners enhance their chances of success. The outcome of the partnership may be impacted by external factors, such as take-overs or economic downturns. Sound account management and regular communication between partners also contribute to success.

Payroll giving

Payroll giving is a simple, tax-efficient way in which employees can give through their salary to support a charity or charities of their choice. The company uses a payroll giving agency, such as CAF, which distributes donations to the employees' chosen charities. Many companies offer payroll giving as part of their community programme. It is an easy way for staff to support a good cause and companies often encourage participation by matching staff's donations.

From the charity's perspective it is a great way to secure regular givers and can be promoted to staff as part of a charity of the year adoption. Many charities engage the services of a professional fundraising organisation (PFO) to promote payroll giving or set up a consortium with other charities. Analysing which companies your payroll givers work for may provide you with the opportunity to develop new corporate relationships.

Employee volunteering

Employee volunteering has increased in popularity over recent years. More and more companies are looking to charities to provide volunteering opportunities for their staff. Companies may be looking for one-off team-building opportunities or wish to encourage employees to give their time and expertise in the form of services, which the charity might otherwise have to pay for, such as legal advice, web design or marketing.

Voluntary work for charities brings numerous benefits to the company. Volunteering can generate effective and visible PR, as well as increase knowledge of the issues that face both customers and society as a whole. For instance, if staff are involved with an older people's charity, they may better understand the issues older people face and improve their services and products accordingly.

A survey of over 200 top businesses revealed that 94 per cent think volunteering adds significantly to the skills of their workforce, particularly in the areas of communication skills, organisation and time management, and people skills.[7] As well as providing the opportunity to do something different from the normal working day, such activity can add value to wider community investment programmes and supplement financial support.

For the charity, providing volunteering opportunities could open doors and lead to a longer-term relationship. It can also generate positive PR for the charity and can be a cost-effective way of adding value to services and other aspects of the charity's work.

Key principles

• Employee volunteering must be of genuine benefit to the charity. Volunteers should be doing a job that needs to be done: avoid creating opportunities just for the sake of it.

• The charity is providing a service to the company wishing to volunteer. Companies can use this as part of their HR strategy, encouraging team building and the acquisition of new skills. It is recommended that the charity seeks financial support from the company to provide such opportunities. There are instances where providing a volunteering

7 TimeBank volunteering survey, 2000, and US conference board survey, 1998.

opportunity for a company opens doors and the potential long-term value of the relationship may make it acceptable to offer the opportunity for free.

● The volunteering must be well managed and the charity must provide support to the volunteers, including clear policies and practices.

Types of volunteering companies are looking for

● **Professional** – using professional expertise for the benefit of the charity; for example, in branding, design, IT, legal. This can be viewed as one-off or ongoing pro bono work or may involve a longer-term secondment.

● **Practical** – helping with a practical need with the aim of producing a tangible end result; for example, redeveloping a piece of land, or decorating a day centre. These types of opportunities, often the most sought after, involve a one-off commitment. Companies often use them as team-building exercises and they are popular as employees can see the tangible impact of their efforts.

● **Personal** – using personal qualities and giving time. This may not require specific professional skills but often requires a longer-term commitment; for example, mentoring, or visiting people in care homes or hospitals. These activities can be the most rewarding and have the most impact in terms of developing employees' skills and experience.

Gifts in kind

A company may not wish to provide monetary support to the charity but may offer support in the form of gifts in kind. For example, a company upgrading its IT system may be willing to donate its old computers to the charity, or a catering company may be willing to provide catering at a charity event for a reduced rate.

It is important when accepting gifts in kind that the charity actually needs what is being offered and that it is of a standard which can be used. This form of support benefits the charity as it can help to reduce costs; for the company it is a way to support a good cause at minimum cost.

Summary

There are numerous ways in which charities can work with companies for mutual benefit, from traditional corporate donations to employee fundraising and commercial tie-ups. The key to all these mechanisms is careful research, building relationships, planning and preparation, monitoring and evaluation.

CHAPTER FOUR

Developing new business

Josephine Job

Choosing the right company

Research

The role of research within corporate fundraising is one of the most important aspects of the job. Any company being approached for support will expect the fundraiser to have done their homework and understand their business needs and objectives.

Some larger charities will have a research department and their main function, in the context of corporate fundraising, will be to identify market trends, understand what the competition are doing, seek out best practice and match up funding opportunities with the needs of the charity. The information gathered by a research department should help direct the energies of the corporate fundraiser department and ensure resources are being used effectively to achieve fundraising targets.

When it comes to deciding which companies to target for funding, the information available in the public domain is only the tip of the iceberg. It is up to the corporate fundraiser to tease out as much information about a potential partner as possible before making the first approach.

When researching the suitability of a corporate partner there are several things that need be taken into consideration;

- Does the company comply with the charity's ethical policy?

- Does the charity have an affinity with the company's brand/product/business objectives?

- Can the charity help the company achieve their objectives while achieving their own?

- Why would they want to partner with one charity over any other?

- What could the charity offer them in return for their investment, for example, access to supporters/service users/members/stakeholders?

- Does the charity have the right PR team and commercial know-how to support a corporate partnership?

● Would the charity be willing to invest enough resource to make the partnership work?

● Could the charity offer them the opportunity to support 'in kind' as well as financially? What volunteering/secondment opportunities would be available to them?

Each corporate decision-making process is unique to that company, but it can often be external factors that have the most influence on their decision to work with a charity, including demands from sector regulators, government social agendas and corporate social responsibility trends. Research launched by Charities Aid Foundation in December 2006 found that all of the top 30 giving companies invest in education, with youth-related and environmental causes in second and third place at 93 per cent and 80 per cent respectively (source: CAF Corporate Community Investment [CCI] study).

Companies will adapt their Corporate Social Responsibility (CSR) strategies and budgets to fit with their ever changing business needs and often this is the first area to be scrutinised when a company's profits are down. Therefore, finding out what their current policy is may require a bit more research.

There are many sources of information available which will help identify the right companies to approach (see Appendix Four, page 188).

Identifying the right contact

Often fundraisers can waste time with a company if they are not dealing with the decision-maker. Identifying who that person is will depend on what the charity wants from the company and what opportunities have been identified during the research process.

If the charity's fundraising strategy is to generate corporate income through the traditional routes of charity of the year, company trusts, or other forms of application-based funding, then the process for identifying the right person to speak to, in the main, should be straightforward as most of this information can be found on a company's website.

However, many companies do not have a CSR department or a process for applying for funding, and in these instances it can be helpful to speak to their PR or advertising departments. Another approach could be through the managing director's PA. They will often know what's going on with their company's community activity and can point you in the right direction of the decision-maker.

However, if the charity's strategy is to approach a company with a bespoke partnership idea that doesn't sit within the usual realms of a CSR department, often the best place to start is with the Marketing Director or alternatively the Managing Director of the company. Decisions made at director level will usually mean compliance from the rest of the organisation and may, in the long term, make it easier to develop the relationship with other key people within the company.

Marketing departments are often more ready to listen to new investment ideas which might give them the upper hand over their competitors. If the company is experienced in CSR, they may even join up their marketing strategy with their CSR strategy. There is evidence in the market place that this is already beginning to happen.

At an Institute of Fundraising Conference in April 2006, Manni Amadi, chief executive of cause&effect, stated that marketing departments within companies are increasingly active in the decision-making of charity partners as companies are now viewing their donations as investments and are actively looking for tangible business benefits.

An ongoing issue faced by corporate fundraisers is that, by the time they have identified the company they want to approach for funding, the company has already committed its CSR budget and is working with its chosen charity of the year for the next X number of years. This should not stop a company from developing partnerships with other charities, if the fundraiser can demonstrate an affinity with the company's business objectives, but they have to be able to show this effectively in their business case. This is often where relationships with marketing departments can be useful. Again, if the charity can identify the right hook for a company it can be easier to sell it their ideas.

A corporate fundraiser's job is to use initiative and identify opportunities that are not necessarily there for everyone to see. They have to be able to turn those opportunities into ideas and sell them to a company. This is what makes a good corporate fundraiser a great corporate fundraiser. They have to be able to identify the right decision-maker within the company that will help deliver the charity's objectives.

A valuable route to the right person within a company might be through the charity's own staff and trustees contacts. Often this is an area that is neglected in the search for the right contact. Their own staff and trustees may know someone influential who works for a company with which they are trying to develop a relationship and it is possible that they might be able to arrange a meeting with that person. It is often surprising who they know and how much influence they have. This is an opportunity that should not be ignored.

Engaging the company in the charity

There is wide debate on the best way to engage a company with a charity. One approach is simply to pick up the phone and make an appointment. It is up to the fundraiser to identify the 'hook' that will make the person want to see them. One way to do this would be to find out what the key issues currently affecting the company or sector are and make this relevant in the approach to the person they want to see. For example, if the company is launching a new product and the demographics of the charity's supporters/recipients is the right audience to market that product to, then this may be the hook, which will get the fundraiser in the door. However, not all charities are comfortable with marketing a company's products to their supporter/recipient database. The fundraiser needs to be clear on what their charity's policy is before approaching a company to support in this way.

Another way of engaging a company may be through the charity's own supporter events. These may not be fundraising events but purely an opportunity for potential supporters to be introduced to the charity. By ensuring a mix of potential and existing supporters at the events, companies will be able to see first hand how much a charity's current partners value their relationship. This may help build the charity's reputation and credentials with potential supporters and may help hook the company in to supporting the charity long term as opposed to purely giving a one off donation.

An alternative approach is for the fundraiser to attend corporate sector events. These may be the company's own industry award ceremonies or selected Business in the Community events. It is useful for any corporate fundraiser to attend these events as it is often an opportunity to get in front of key decision-makers.

Finally, although this approach is not widely used by fundraisers it is possible to ask existing supporters if they would be willing to set up a meeting with a potential supporter if they have the right contacts. This is not unheard of if your fundraiser has a good relationship with the existing supporter.

Developing corporate relationships

Raising the charity's profile

Another aspect of a corporate fundraiser's role is to raise the profile of their charity within the voluntary and corporate social responsibility arena.

There are various ways of achieving this. One way is to develop a robust marketing plan, which will target the various CSR consultants and PR agencies that influence companies' CSR activities.

Research from the Ingenious Group published in 2004 stated that only 12 per cent of cold approaches to companies from charities are successful and 75 per cent of relationships are developed by the company approaching the charity. This research also shows that 13 per cent of partnerships were developed through third parties including PR agencies and consultancy firms specialising in corporate social responsibility.

It is a key ingredient of the success of any corporate fundraising strategy to establish the right relationships with key influencers such as PR/advertising agencies, CSR consultants, voluntary sector publication editors/journalists and third-sector suppliers. They can often help to get the fundraiser's name known and will add credibility to them and their organisation as a potential partner.

It is common practice for companies to employ external CSR consultants to advise them on their policies and to identify causes that will create a greater connection between their community affairs and marketing activity – in other words, to develop a strategy that has a proper fit with their business objectives and demonstrates an affinity with their brand. It is possible to join these agencies' membership schemes, which will offer access to their corporate members and can provide an opportunity to meet the right contacts.

Nurturing individual relationships

Being a corporate fundraiser means learning to be patient and knowing how to build up trust between yourself and the key contact. The fundraiser has to be able to demonstrate their charity's commitment to the partnership before the charity can begin to reap the rewards of the relationship. It is really important to understand this if the charity wants to develop long-term, lucrative relationships with companies.

Finding out what it is that makes the person tick will demonstrate to them that the fundraiser is interested in meeting their objectives as well as their own. A way of achieving this is to listen to what they have to say about their role within the organisation and what they are expected to achieve. If they are asking for information, find out what format they would like to receive this in. Make their relationship with the charity as easy as possible. The more information known about a person, the easier it is to give them what they want.

It is important to develop trust in any relationship, even more so when money and reputation are involved. The key contact has to be able to trust that the fundraiser can deliver what they say and feel confident they can work with them towards a successful and fulfilling partnership. It will often have been their decision to choose the charity partner, so their reputation within the company will depend on delivering a successful outcome.

It is possible to secure a few 'quick wins' but these are often not sustainable and long-term partnerships are what a corporate fundraiser should always be aiming for. Longer-term, multi-year project funding will provide a charity with secured revenue over a number of years.

It can take anything from six to eighteen months for a corporate relationship to come to fruition and often the donations or support will be small scale until the company is comfortable with the relationship. It is usually only then that multi-year support will be on the table.

Proposals and pitching

Written proposals

If a company has an established charity-giving policy they will often have a template application form to complete which will have set criteria. If this is not the case, there is a suggested formula that can be used when submitting written proposals. This includes defining what the charity's beneficiaries' issues are (demonstrating the need), what the charity is doing to provide a solution, how the company can help with that solution (what the charity wants from them) and what is in it for them in return for their investment.

If the company is being asked to fund a project, what will be the exit strategy once funding has run out? How will the charity show sustainability of the project? How will they measure the impact of the partnership and report back?

The way in which this information is presented will rely on how well the fundraiser knows the company. The information which has been gleaned while developing their relationship will help enormously in pitching the proposal at the right level.

Companies are not keen on receiving written proposals on spec. They will expect a charity to discuss their ideas with them first before submitting a proposal. This is also good practice for the charity as it will save time and money in the long run and will help the charity to focus its corporate fundraising activity.

If it is a traditional application-based fundraising approach, then often a proposal will be the first stage of the pitching process. However, if it is a bespoke approach, best practice states that a proposal should be the last part of the process in securing income, not the first.

Written proposals can also be used to formalise the outcomes of discussions with a company and can form the basis for letters of agreement, should both parties agree to proceed with the partnership.

The pitching process

Irrespective of what the charity is pitching to a company it is essential to understand the audience they are pitching to. Communicating ideas/proposals to them in a format that they recognise and understand is a key ingredient for delivering a successful pitch.

It is important to be clear about what the charity wants from the company and what they are going to give them in return for their investment. Sticking to the brief that has been given will demonstrate that the charity understands what is being asked of them. The corporate fundraiser should be prepared to ask questions if the information they require is not included in the brief. It is better to be completely prepared and cover as many bases as possible before the day of the pitch.

The pitch is the charity's opportunity to bring their ideas to life. Company feedback on charity pitches indicates that the ones that stand out are those that have been creative in their approach and been truly enthusiastic about their ideas. There is no harm in putting a bit of energy in a pitch. If the fundraiser believes in what they are selling, other people will too.

Concentrating on mutual benefit and how both parties can work together to deliver joint objectives is key, as is being able to demonstrate the charity's unique selling point which will help them to stand out from the competition.

It is important to be able to demonstrate impact for both organisations' key stakeholders. Continuing to show mutual benefit throughout the pitch will highlight the affinity between the two organisations.

The charity needs to show the company how they will support the partnership. This goes back to understanding what the company wants. If it is a high-profile campaign and they expect national media coverage, how is the charity going to deliver this? Does the charity have the right PR resources to support a national campaign and provide the level of coverage that the company expects? This is something the charity needs to think about before getting to pitch stage.

One thing that charities need to consider when pitching to national companies is the level of support the company may expect from the partnership. There are various aspects of a corporate relationship that demand resources from the charity, so if corporate fundraisers have included benefits to a company in their pitch the charity needs to be able to support this. If not, it can be damaging to the reputation of the charity within the corporate sector and will most definitely affect the success of repeat business from the company.

Other benefits that a company may expect to hear during a pitch are how their staff might get involved in the partnership. If the idea is a CRM campaign, how will the charity help sell more products via their communication channels. How might this impact on their sales figures and brand awareness?

It is best practice to provide case studies of existing corporate partnerships, preferably within the same sector as the company being approached. This will add credibility to the pitch and demonstrate the charity's experience as a partner.

A key main issue facing charities is the time and money that their corporate fundraisers can spend on corporate pitches. However, this investment is essential if the charity wants to win the business. Corporate fundraisers will be expected to put the same time and effort into pitching for new business as any other sales team approaching a company for business. However, strategic consideration needs to be given to balancing investment with potential return. With such a high number of companies running charity of the year schemes, it is tempting for fundraisers to feel they need to be applying for each and every one available. A clear process needs to be in place to assess potential success and for time investment to be allocated accordingly. Corporate fundraising is high risk and there are no guarantees that because the charity gets to pitching stage they will be successful. A charity has to decide whether or not they are willing to take this risk. If they do the rewards can be well worth the investment.

Summary

Corporate partnerships are all about building relationships with key contacts within a company. The best way to do this is to meet face to face and to build up a picture of individual motivations in addition to corporate objectives.

Time should be allowed to develop the relationship to the stage where asking for money becomes a natural next step. This will ensure the charity's expertise is trusted and valued.

If corporate partnerships are to reach their potential, charities need to be willing to invest time and resources to develop long-term, mutually beneficial partnerships.

CHAPTER FIVE

Developing and managing corporate partnerships in the 21st century

Andrew Peel

This chapter takes a pragmatic look at how charities can maximise the opportunities presented by the new climate of corporate responsibility that has emerged in recent years. By better understanding their potential attraction to business partners, packaging their causes and brands in the best possible way and developing impactful strategies, most – if not all – charities can deliver outstanding results from private-sector partnerships.

A new paradigm for corporate responsibility

As the spotlight on corporations intensifies and scrutiny from customers, the media, non-governmental organisations, employees, shareholders and other stakeholders increases, so companies have had little option but to take a long, hard look at their overall impact on society.

Most commentators agree that, in addition to increasing profits, the most important thing a company can do now is to be seen as 'socially responsible' in a particular market – whether that means donations to charity, investment in the community, production of safe, high-quality products, protection of the environment or treating employees fairly.

The result of this sea-change for charities has been a clear shift in companies' focus from traditional philanthropy towards relationships of a more strategic nature – a move, in other words, from donations towards investment and a desire for tangible business benefits to come out of such associations. While it is excellent news on one level, this change in emphasis has significantly increased the scale of the task facing those charities targeting the corporate sector for income. Corporate alliances can be extremely rewarding on many levels, even for small charities and niche causes, but they also present such organisations with a unique set of challenges and potential pitfalls.

New climate, new tactics

Although we are arguably in a better position than ever before to broker new alliances with the corporate sector, charities still need to hone their approach if they are to enjoy sustained levels of success. Clear vision and strategic planning are the keys to realising your ambitions. What follows, therefore, is a step-by-step guide to developing a well-measured and coherent approach to your strategy that can be revisited and adapted as necessary.

Step 1: Articulating your vision

Your starting point for outlining the direction of your team must be to paint a picture of what the future will look like. It needs to be something that encapsulates the opportunity and the goal, inspires, appeals to your team and the wider charity, is feasible, flexible and focused and, ideally, something that can be easily explained in a few minutes. (See Appendix Two, page 175 for an example of how a corporate fundraising vision can feed into the strategy.)

Step 2: Analysing your situation

The next step in developing your strategy is to take stock of where you are now, understand your strengths and your weaknesses and begin to scope out a strategy for expanding your business. There are numerous tools available for helping you define your strategic approach, but experience has shown that the following five are invaluable in answering the key questions and informing your priorities.

1 SWOT analysis

The trusty old SWOT (Strengths, Weaknesses, Opportunities and Threats) analysis helps you very quickly understand your organisation's core competencies – or lack of them. It can help you identify opportunities that you may be in a position to take advantage of, and, by highlighting your organisation's and/or your department's weaknesses, you can plan how you will avoid or cope with potentially damaging threats. Furthermore, by looking at yourself *and* your competitors, you can start to develop a strategy that helps to set you apart from others in your market.

2 PESTLE analysis

This other well-used tool helps you gain clarity about which external factors could affect your organisation's ability to achieve its mission. PESTLE analysis (which considers external Political, Economic, Social, Technological, Legal and Environmental issues or influences) helps you develop a clearer sense of likely future events, and the competencies you and your team may need in order to achieve your goals.

3 The Boston matrix

The Boston matrix is a simple analytical tool, devised by Boston Consulting, which helps you visualise the probable life-cycle of your projects, products, clients, donors (plus colleagues and trustees if necessary!). It will help you identify your so-called *Cash Cows*, *Rising Stars*, *Sick Children* and your *Dead Dogs* – thereby highlighting not only which aspects of your current corporate strategy/portfolio yield the best return on investment (ROI), but also those which are likely to require more attention and investment of resources in the future (and of course those initiatives probably best left to wither and die). It will also help you understand which fundraising techniques or 'products' your team will need to use in the future – be that payroll giving, direct mail, employee fundraising, cause-related marketing or events.

4 The Ansoff matrix

The Ansoff matrix is a tool devised in the 1950s by H. Igor Ansoff that provides a useful focus around which debate in your team can take place, as it helps you decide how and where to expand your activities. In a very market-/customer-focused way, it helps you identify all your current products/offerings and their markets, and makes you consider growth strategies – whether you should be targeting *new or existing markets* with *new or existing products*.

5 Common sense

Finally, do not forget to take an objective look at where you are. Having tried some of these analytical tools, do take a few steps back at the end of the process and review the bigger picture. If your various brainstorms, grids and matrices are telling you one thing, but your instinct is telling you another, do take a closer look at the outputs. While there is a chance you may be wrong, remember that you know far more about your organisation than Messrs Boston and Ansoff!

Step 3: Tightening your strategic focus

Having both formulated a clear vision for the development of your corporate fundraising function and acquired a sense of your organisation's strengths, vulnerabilities and ability to deal (or not deal) with external factors, you should now have a good feel for the direction in which your new strategy must take you.

The range of hooks upon which to hang your strategy will now probably look something like this:

- **'Maximise the potential of existing relationships and fulfil all contractual obligations'** – The fact that you have a new strategic plan should not impact negatively upon the important corporate relationships already on your books. If you're only half way through a three-year partnership, for example, be careful not to lose sight of your commitments to that client. Pay particular heed to the Pareto principle which, when applied to fundraising, holds that 80 per cent of your support is likely to come from 20 per cent of your customers or donors. Your existing clients are your most important ones. Remember, it is far more resource-intensive to bring on board a new client or supporter than retain or develop an old one.

- **'Develop new fundraising/marketing activities with current corporate supporters'** – It's likely that it will be more effective to develop new income streams from existing supporters than to rely heavily upon researching and securing new business relationships from scratch. A key objective for your team, therefore, may be to look at ways of upgrading existing levels of support by promoting established fundraising mechanisms or products.

- **'Develop new relationships through existing networks'** – There may well be informal opportunities for doing this – by talking to your trustees or existing corporate supporters and by endeavouring to gain access to their contacts or networks; or formal ones – such as by establishing a fundraising appeal board or corporate panel.

- **'Attract new corporate supporters'** – Whether your corporate fundraising function is new or has enjoyed many years of success, you will need to give consideration to how you will attract new supporters to your cause. If you have exhausted your corporate contacts and networks, this will inevitably involve researching business sectors which have clear synergies with your work and brand.

Let us take the example of an international eye care charity. The corporate fundraising manager might map out all the potential industries and sectors which arguably have a relevance to, or resonance with, the charity's work as shown in Figure 5.1.

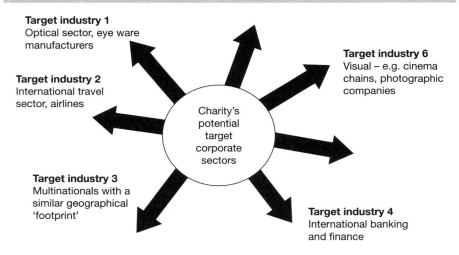

FIGURE 5.1 TARGET INDUSTRIES RELEVANT TO THE WORK OF AN EYE CARE CHARITY

Target industry 1
Optical sector, eye ware manufacturers

Target industry 2
International travel sector, airlines

Target industry 3
Multinationals with a similar geographical 'footprint'

Charity's potential target corporate sectors

Target industry 6
Visual – e.g. cinema chains, photographic companies

Target industry 4
International banking and finance

Step 4: Adopting the right mindset and management style

Those corporate fundraising managers who fail to plan, fail to invest adequately in their teams, neglect to carry out adequate research into their prospective partners, fail to assess potential risk or are unable to adopt a hard-nosed, business-orientated approach to their partnerships ultimately stand little chance of success. The following 'golden rules' have therefore been drawn up to help you navigate a course through the complex maze that is corporate fundraising.

Team structure

Much has been written about the pros and cons of the different approaches to structuring corporate fundraising teams, and unfortunately there is very little agreement about which is best. The truth is, there is no 'right' way or 'wrong' way to do it. The way you go about managing your team and its work will be down to a combination of factors such as personal preference, the size of your organisation and budget, and the number of relationships already on the books. All that really matters is that the structure enables you to deliver against your strategy, that you review the structure regularly to ensure it is working for you and that you, as the manager and team leader, are clear about who is responsible for what.

Drawing on personal experience from a number of charities, the author has found the following approaches all work well in the right situation.

- **Jack of All Trades approach** – with one specialist corporate fundraiser in a team of fundraisers. This is the usual approach for small and medium-sized charities in which corporate fundraising is a relatively new and/or undeveloped discipline. The trick for the manager here is to be able to gauge when this individual is reaching capacity and needs additional support.

- **All Hands on Deck approach** – with a team of perhaps three or four account handlers, each of whom has responsibility for a mixed portfolio of corporate accounts and new business generation.

- **Two Tribes approach** – with a separate new business or development function *plus* a team of account handlers managing the existing and ensuing business partnerships. In larger charities, there will often be an extra tier, with account handlers reporting to one, two or even three senior corporate fundraisers.

- **Sector-focused approach** – with a New Business team plus a large team of account handlers focusing on specific sectors, such as supermarkets, finance, pharmaceuticals. This opens the door for the recruitment of staff with specialist knowledge of a particular sector, a move which can, in itself, lead to a significant up-turn in income.

- **Product-focused approach** – with a team of account handlers in which there is a clear division between 'commercial' account specialists (focusing on CRM, affinity marketing, e-commerce, licensing, sponsorship and other trading activity) and 'non-commercial' or 'philanthropic' account handlers (focusing on such areas as philanthropic support, employee fundraising, charity of the year relationships, corporate direct mail, payroll giving). Additionally, in larger or international charities, you may find it helpful to segment your team's work along other lines so that there is a clear division (for example) between UK corporate opportunities and multinational relationships.

- **Central vs Regional approach.** If you have a corporate fundraising team at head office, you may have to put in place (or you may inherit) a structure which dovetails with your regional fundraising strategy, perhaps the fundraising contributions of volunteers, and, in larger charities, the work of regional corporate fundraisers. The challenge here is to find an approach that enables all fundraisers to work to one joined-up national strategy, which avoids the dreaded turf wars and which enables fundraisers to meet their own income targets. The best solution the author has come across to this conundrum was at the British Red Cross, where regional corporate fundraisers and community fundraisers were encouraged to work together for the 'greater good' through the use of finders' fees, soft-crediting and regular dialogue.

- **Managing the Big One.** If you are fortunate enough to land a major account, such as an adoption by one of the big supermarket chains, you will almost certainly need to restructure and possibly recruit additional staff if you are going to cope with the increased workload and make the most of the opportunities such a tie-up can present.

Team systems

Databases and 'customer' relationship management

Fundraising databases have many functions, but their key role is to improve your fundraising and your efficiency, and thus your bottom line. In many respects, an efficient central fundraising database or customer relationship management system is a vital marketing tool. And the larger the charity, the greater the need for an efficient marketing tool that can be accessed and understood by all staff.

While space does not permit a detailed analysis of the role of databases in fundraising, it is important to understand why they are such an essential tool for corporate fundraisers:

- They provide the means to record simple corporate donor or prospect information, giving fundraisers a clear overview of a donor's giving and contact history, and other important material information.

- They facilitate information exchange across the team, department or organisation, and are particularly useful for enabling colleagues to see which account handler or 'key worker' has responsibility for which corporate account.

- They allow vital cross-referencing of donor information – flagging, for instance, where a corporate contact has also become a major donor, or perhaps where a volunteer is a major legator.

- They enable the production of income reports – at month or year end, for example, or perhaps for the analysis of particular campaigns, corporate mailings or donor giving histories.

- They enable you to segment and 'de-dupe' your data, thereby helping you to experiment with different fundraising and mailing strategies until the optimum result is achieved.

- They provide a means of generating standard thank you and other appeal letters with the minimum of effort.

The key issue from a corporate fundraising perspective is that your fundraising database must be able to handle a wide range of complex information and interrelationships. It needs to work for the charity's corporate fundraisers, community or regional fundraisers, major donor fundraisers, events organisers and direct marketers – enabling them to cross-reference company and individuals' giving histories and preferences, tap into relevant research and pick up on other vital, sensitive data in a bid to get a clear picture and plan their approach.

Databases inevitably come in all shapes and sizes, but the best advice on the subject is:

First, buy the best product that your budget will allow, that is appropriate for your size of charity, is implemented by a company with a track record in the sector, and which provides appropriate service levels and customer care. Second, ensure that your organisation is prepared to invest in staff training on the system, particularly for those colleagues who may be based away from head office. There's no point having a database costing you several thousand pounds if only a select few know how to use it. And finally, ensure that any organisational database purchased by your charity is going to be compatible with the corporate fundraising one, and vice versa.

Securing internal buy-in

Corporate fundraising will never succeed if it operates in a vacuum. It is absolutely crucial that you have internal buy-in, particularly among your senior management team and the trustees, because it is they who will ultimately be the key to future expansion and investment – be that in a new database, training, consultants or additional staff when the time is right. They can also have a key role to play in terms of fronting approaches to companies and using their network of contacts to open doors for your team (though you may find they need some gentle coaxing to do this!)

But there are other key colleagues that you must get on side too, since you will inevitably be dependent upon them for support and advice if you land a demanding corporate partnership. Colleagues with whom you will need to work most closely are likely to include: the communications/PR/ press team, the website coordinator, the finance function and of course, those who are implementing the charity's work.

There are several techniques for doing this, including, for example:

• arranging one-to-one meetings to talk colleagues through your strategy, the 'bigger picture', and explore how you might tap into their expertise in the future;

• inviting the whole organisation to an informal briefing about your work, plans, successes and failures, giving them the opportunity to get to know your team over tea and biscuits;

• or perhaps inviting key colleagues along to meetings with companies where their expertise will prove invaluable and which will lead to them feeling engaged in the relationship.

One inevitable consequence of working in corporate fundraising is that there will always be a small number of colleagues who do not support you, mainly for 'ethical' reasons and because they believe that the charity should not be engaging with the private sector. All you can do is be ready for this, ensure that they understand the reasons why you are doing what you're doing (to generate more income to enable the charity to achieve its mission) and that your team has a responsible, well-measured, 'ethical' approach to working with companies.

Remember: small is beautiful

It is perfectly feasible for your organisation – regardless of its size or how niche or complex your cause – to broker successful partnerships with blue-chip companies. Major corporate partnerships do not have to be the sole preserve of the big, household name charities. In fact, a small, lean charity with limited political baggage and bureaucracy could be just what a company is looking for in a partner. Why not ask them which they would prefer? Anything is possible in this arena if you think big enough, have done your homework properly and have the courage to go for it.

At the same time, it may be that the pursuit of larger companies and more onerous types of partnership is not the best option for your charity at this point. There is perhaps a greater argument for you focusing on the smaller opportunities that lie within your grasp, honing your skills and delivering on your promises with less risk attached – and then look to build on these foundations. Remember, too, that there are more than a million small and medium-sized enterprises (SMEs) in the UK, the vast majority of which will never have been asked to support a charity in any strategic or mutually beneficial way.

Consider collaboration, not competition

The charities that will reap the greatest rewards in the coming years will be the ones that not only look carefully at what assets they have and package them effectively – but also those that are prepared to actually engage with their competitors. There is clearly a lot more that could be achieved if the vast numbers of voluntary organisations with similar objectives in the same field came together more often and engaged with the corporate sector as one united force for change. With this approach, we could, as a sector, generate higher levels of income, set more ambitious targets and make a far greater impact on the world. For me, that represents the perfect vision of the future of corporate partnerships.

CHAPTER SIX

Getting the measure of corporate community investment

Ita McMahon and Mike Tuffrey

Many companies working closely with community partners on corporate community investment (CCI) already track their contributions to charitable projects – be it cash, time or in-kind donations. Not satisfied with putting a figure on their company-wide CCI input, progressive businesses are now going one step further and are increasingly considering what their community programmes actually achieve. This shift in emphasis has implications for fundraisers and not-for-profit project managers alike, as the task of measuring the outputs and long-term impacts of community projects, existing or potential, cannot be carried out by a corporate community affairs department alone. Increasingly, businesses are turning to their community partners for evidence that their projects have been successful. Partnerships are also under scrutiny to ensure that prospective projects have robust frameworks for reporting results. In fact, some companies now ask potential community partners to submit proposals following the London Benchmarking Group (LBG) model of input/leverage/output/ impact. Consequently, the need to agree goals and measurement metrics at a project's outset has never been greater.

In this context, this chapter aims to 1) give community partners insight into the reasons for the corporate focus on CCI measurement; 2) explain the LBG model, used by 150 leading companies worldwide to determine their company's voluntary contribution to the community; and 3) outline some guiding principles on how fundraisers and not-for-profit project managers can respond effectively to the corporate need for measurement.

The importance of measuring

There are many reasons why businesses are now measuring their community investment programmes. Measurement can inform management decisions, improve performance and help businesses to anticipate problems and respond effectively. Input and output measurement also enables

47

comparisons across projects and verification that programme objectives have been achieved.

In particular, there are three easily identifiable reasons why companies are focusing on project results and not just input costs[8].

1 Measurement shifts the debate from costs to benefits.

By only reporting the inputs to community activities, programmes tend to be seen as a cost, rather than a benefit to the company. Measuring and reporting community and business benefits puts the costs into proper perspective. Senior managers will accept sizable upfront project costs if they think the benefits are worthwhile, and are more willing approve larger sums if they see it as an investment with returns to the business and the community.

2 Output reporting gives the true measure of what is contributed.

Reporting input costs also seriously undervalues the corporate contribution to the community. This is particularly true for smaller businesses and individual operating units within larger companies where the monetary input value to project may be small, but the resulting impact on the local community is significant. Moreover, output measurement encourages companies to capture leverage, the additional funds unlocked by a company's financial support, as well as community and business benefits of the CCI progamme.

3 Efficiency and effectiveness are improved.

Analysing CCI enables companies to make management decisions about efficiency and effectiveness of a scheme based on the best possible outcomes for the level of contribution. The aim is to invest in community projects that have a high rate of return for a reasonable input cost. This helps to ensure that community involvement will grow across the business, even when central giving budgets are flat or declining.

So, how do businesses go about measuring the costs and benefits of their community involvement? One approach is through LBG. LBG is both a benchmarking group where member companies share data and best practice, and a model that provides a framework for measuring the inputs and outputs of community investment.

8 Logan, D. and Tuffrey, M. *Companies in Communities: Assessing the Impact,* Charities Aid Foundation, 2000, 14-15.

London Benchmarking Group (LBG)

The LBG model is used by hundreds of leading businesses around the world and LBG has centres in a growing number of key world markets including Australia, Canada, the Czech Republic, Germany and the USA. Members include multinationals such as Cadbury Schweppes, HSBC, Vodafone and Unilever, as well as major UK companies such as Marks & Spencer and BSkyB. The key achievement of the benchmarking group has been to establish a common definition for community involvement, for the valuation of inputs and the measuring of outputs.

In the early 1990s, companies wishing to measure their activity in the community suffered from a lack of common definitions, inconsistent approaches, poor data on the cost of contributions and little evaluation of what was being achieved.

In response to these needs, six leading UK-based companies (BP, Diageo, IBM, Marks & Spencer, NatWest Group and Whitbread) came together in 1994 to examine how they manage and measure their community involvement programmes, seeking to learn from each other and explore common definitions and performance measures.

Then in 1997, the original six were joined by another 12 (American Express, BT, Camelot, Centrica, Levi Strauss, Nationwide Building Society, News International, Railtrack, Rio Tinto, GlaxoSmithKline, Unilever and United Utilities). Representing a broad spread of industry sectors, they funded a new initiative to refine further the measurement techniques and to promote the approach widely in the UK and abroad. This work was undertaken by the CSR management consultancy the Corporate Citizenship Company and supported by the Charities Aid Foundation (CAF).

The third stage of LBG's development was to roll out membership to any company interested in measuring community investment. Over 100 major UK firms are now LBG members, and membership worldwide reaches 150 companies. LBG is now in its '4G' (fourth generation), where a key aim is to measure outputs from the whole programme budget, not just flagships, and moving to assess long-term impacts from major investment.

This is where community organisations must step up to the challenge of measuring and monitoring results of partnership projects on the ground. This could be through monitoring the number of young people helped, the effect on healthcare standards, or whichever metric is appropriate for that project. The not-for-profit sector must also seriously consider ways of monitoring the impact of long-term projects, and add real value and meaning to partnerships by reporting back. The LBG model provides an ideal framework for this.

The LBG model – inputs

The starting point of the London Benchmarking Group model is the range of motivations for corporate community involvement, covering:

• a sense of moral and social responsibility, also responding to expectations from society for community involvement;

• a belief that companies have a long-term interest in fostering a healthy community, sometimes known as enlightened self-interest;

• the knowledge that community interventions involving employees, customers and suppliers can have direct benefits, through increased profitability, stronger company image, reduced costs, better employee morale and improved customer loyalty.

In the LBG model, these three motivations are represented in the top three sections of the triangle in Figure 6.1. Under these headings, the London Benchmarking Group has created a unique template for companies to measure and manage the input side of individual community activities. The model goes beyond traditional charitable giving by including employee time and in-kind donations. It provides clear definitions for each type of activity, specifying how the costs incurred (inputs) are to be valued. It also acknowledges that the costs of managing community relations must be included. The solid line in the diagram represents the voluntary contributions by which companies are judged in LBG. However, it is important to recognize that mandatory contributions and business basics are a significant part of the total impact a company has on society. Mandatory contributions include services to disadvantaged customers that energy providers are required to provide as a condition of their licence to operate; the social impact of business basics includes jobs created; and taxes paid.

When companies first apply the model on the input side, they often have to make judgements about when an activity counts towards the community contribution and when it is really part of business basics, so whether it falls above or below the solid line in the diagram above. The utilities sector, in particular, needs to distinguish between 'community' expenditure required by industry regulators and genuine voluntary contributions, often in the area of customers with special needs. United Utilities, for example, has a broad programme of support for 'extra needs' customers, provided by the business, but goes beyond regulator requirements with further activity through the community programme.

FIGURE 6.1 THE LBG MODEL

The LBG model

Charitable gifts

Intermittent support to a wide range of good causes in response to the needs and appeals of charitable and community organisations. Increasingly through partnerships between the company, its employees, customers and suppliers.

Community investment

Long-term strategic involvement in community partnerships to address a limited range of social issues chosen by the company in order to protect its long-term corporate interests and to enhance its reputation.

Commercial initiatives in the community

Activities in the community, usually by commercial departments, to support directly the success of the company, promoting its corporate brand identities and other policies, in partnership with charities and community-based organisations.

Mandatory contributions

Community contributions or activities undertaken as a result of the requirements of law, regulation or contact.

Business basics

The core business activities in meeting society's needs for cost effective goods and services in a manner which is ethically, socially and environmentally responsible.

The LBG matrix – outputs and impacts

The LBG model allows a more comprehensive valuation of the 'input' cost but it also goes further, to cover what the programme actually achieves. Outputs are plotted on a matrix against input costs, as shown in the LBG matrix in Figure 6.2. The output and impact sections of the model are the areas in which community organisations can add real value by reporting back to their corporate partner the immediate results and longer term effects of their projects.

Outputs are defined in terms of:

• leverage of cash and resources from other sources drawn in by the programme;

• the community benefit, such as the number of people in society who benefit;

• the business benefit which accrues.

Examples of leverage include the cash generated from a marketing campaign on behalf of a charity or government funds attracted to a local community by the company contribution. To report effectively on leverage, LBG members are reliant on their community partners for information on the way in which their support has unlocked extra funding or resources. Forward-thinking community organisations should not only investigate and maximise leverage opportunities, but also build leverage reporting into project updates.

FIGURE 6.2 THE LBG MATRIX

Community Activity	INPUTS	OUTPUTS		
	Cash Value	Leverage	Community Benefits	Business Benefits
Charitable Gifts				
Community Investment				
Commercial Initiatives in the Community				

Community impacts	Business impacts

Community benefits is another area where community partners can add real value, first by providing baselines, suitable reporting metrics and goals at a project's outset, and then by regular reporting on progress and achievements. The type of metric will clearly depend on the kind of project, but examples of community benefit include the number of young people gaining jobs from a company-supported training scheme, or the number of people learning IT skills from a CCI computing programme.

Business benefits would include enhanced reputation from a donation and increased sales during a cause-related marketing promotion, but here too, community partners can make a valuable contribution. An obvious example would be to raise awareness with community affairs and HR staff of the skills development available through participation in a community volunteering scheme.

One area of frequent confusion is the difference between the cost to the company of, for example, in-kind donations of goods and the 'opportunity cost' (notional sales income foregone) if the charity had had to purchase the goods on the open market. Some non-LBG member companies use the latter (larger) figure as their contribution, but in the view of the London Benchmarking Group this is incorrect: only the actual cost of manufacturing the goods counts as the input figure; an amount for the worth to the charity, based on a sales price, can be used as an output measure of benefit to the community. Indeed, under the charity SORP (statement of recommended practice) rules, this is the figure normally used in the beneficiary's accounts.

Comparing input costs and outputs achieved between companies allows a judgement to be made about the effectiveness of community involvement programmes. In this way, the LBG model becomes a dynamic management tool.

Example: Vodafone's initial contribution to the Thames Valley Early Intervention Initiative in Banbury was £60,000 over three years plus management costs. The leverage unlocked by Vodafone's involvement totalled £165,000 in government grants and other funding, demonstrating that even a relatively small investment can still generate considerable community benefit.

Beyond outputs are the longer-term effects of the CCI projects, known as 'impacts' in the LBG model. Impacts are inevitably harder to evaluate because of the difficulty in isolating the causes and the longer timescales.

Typically inputs are measured over one year, outputs over one to two years and impacts up to ten. Charitable organisations involved in long-term partnerships with corporate sponsors are in the ideal position to report back on impacts, and many now include the cost of impact monitoring as part of their initial fundraising pitch.

Some leading businesses involved in social projects have begun to calculate the 'social return on investment (SROI)' of community projects. SROI falls into the impacts category of the LBG model. The process starts by assessing the number of people benefiting from the project and uses basic assumptions about the financial effect. So, with certain assumptions in place, it is possible to estimate the social return on investment of a training scheme to get unemployed people into work by calculating the social security costs saved and the tax revenue generated. SROI helps to bolster perceptions that corporate community investment has business and community benefits, rather than expenditure that cannot be recouped.

Example: Over a 20-year period, Diageo and Tomorrow's People Trust have helped more than 380,000 people out of unemployment. Independent research has shown that this has saved the UK economy around £450 million through Job Seeker's Allowance saved, additional tax receipts and reductions in health expenditure and crime.

LBG for community partners

As we have seen, LBG corporate members are now increasingly requiring their community partners to understand the business need to measure results and even to use the LBG model as a framework for measurement and reporting. In response to this demand and with the support of LBG corporate members, we have launched an LBG workshop for community partners to enable charitable organisations to understand the LBG model and to help improve the dialogue between business and their partners.

The LBG model is a helpful tool for community partners. It can be used as a framework for monitoring the inputs, outputs and impacts of specific projects. The matrix can also be used as a communication aid when reporting internally, externally or in pitches to potential partners. Moreover, using the LBG model helps community partners to identify the additional funds that a corporate sponsor's support has unlocked.

The use of the LBG model by community partners is not a new development. In the late 1990s ActionAid used the LBG model in promotional literature to highlight the ways in which it works with corporate partners in each of the motivational categories outlined in Figure 6.1. Under the charitable gifts section, it highlighted some of the companies that contribute cash support and matched employee giving. For community investment, ActionAid highlighted the staff development opportunities available to partner companies through volunteering and secondments. Finally, the section on commercial initiatives in the community described some of the businesses that had partnered ActionAid in cause-related marketing campaigns.

By using the LBG model, ActionAid was able to communicate to a corporate audience the varying means by which a company can get involved and the business benefits arising from such involvement.

Guiding principles on measurement

Regardless of the type of measurement model used, there are some key principles that are applicable across the board. A recent study, published jointly by the Corporate Citizenship Company and Business in the Community, looked beyond voluntary community investment and compiled a toolkit to assess a company's entire contribution to society, from their core products and economic impact through to corporate policies and voluntary community investment. Although the report[9] was devised for a corporate audience, the five key 'dos and don'ts' that the study highlighted are equally relevant to the charitable sector. The hints and tips help to gain greater understanding of the kinds of reporting required by corporate partners and should help those community organisations struggling to measure their programmes.

So why ultimately does CCI measurement matter? A common basis for monitoring, measuring and reporting helps community affairs managers to make the case for expanding and diversifying their activities. Better data allow better management, benefiting business and wider society. The not-for-profit sector, too, will profit, through a greater understanding of what companies can do, how and why. Well-managed and evaluated community programmes are not just more effective, they are sustainable even when resources in the business are under pressure. It is in everyone's interest to get the measure of the community involvement.

9 *More than Making Money: Measuring the Difference Your Company Makes to Society* (2006) Research partners: The Corporate Citizenship Company and Business in the Community; Corporate Partners: BT, Diageo, John Lewis Partnership, KPMG, RWEnpower, Serco Group, Severn Trent and Vodafone.

FIGURE 6.3 PRINCIPLES OF MEASUREMENT – TOP TEN TIPS

do...

1 **Do be clear about your goals before you start measuring.**
This will fundamentally affect the method you chose. Measurement is all about knowing if you are achieving your objectives.

2 **Do identify who is going to use the results, and how.**
Design the process to best meet the differing needs of your various stakeholders.

3 **Do give your stakeholders a voice in the process.**
Capture their views through qualitative as well as quantitative measures. Numbers alone are rarely enough.

4 **Do use a robust methodology and ensure you have concrete evidence to back up your findings.**
Avoid anecdote. Only extrapolate from a single initiative to a 'whole company' conclusion when there is a reliable and credible sampling basis.

5 **Do distinguish between inputs, outputs and impacts, and between measures of process and of results.**
Decide which to measure and what tool to use according to the objectives you have set.

don't...

1 **Don't think measurement alone will improve results.**
Assessment must be integrated into management processes and the results used to inform decisions that will make a difference over time.

2 **Don't over-engineer the process.**
Simple measures may not capture the full complexity but are more likely to be applied, the findings understood and the conclusions acted upon.

3 **Don't always go it alone.**
Consider involving expert third parties for greater credibility. Use recognised techniques so the results can be more easily benchmarked.

4 **Don't communicate positive aspects only.**
Measurement needs to be objective and balanced in order to strengthen credibility.

5 **Don't think you have to measure everything.**
Consider the time and effort against the usability of likely results. Often the process of clarifying goals and identifying performance measures helps to focus activity and achieves better results even without actual measurement. Be willing to say 'no' to measuring for the sake of it.

Reference material

For more information on the London Benchmarking Group and the LBG workshop for community partners, see the LBG website:

http://www.lbg-online.net/

More Than Making Money: Measuring the Difference Your Company Makes to Society, published in 2006 by the Corporate Citizenship Company and Business in the Community, is available online at:

http://www.corporate-citizenship.co.uk/measurement/

Logan, D. and Tuffrey, M. *Companies in Communities: Assessing the* Impact, Charities Aid Foundation, 2000

CHAPTER SEVEN

Take it or leave it
Corporate fundraising ethics

Ian McQuillin

A few years ago I was sitting in on a corporate fundraising session at the Institute of Fundraising convention. We were split into breakout groups and given an exercise to work through. We had to consider whether we would accept a corporate partnership from a brass manufacturing company operating in Brazil. So after we had checked all the possible ethical factors that could be at play, we decided we'd take the cash.

'What if I told you,' said the American consultant running the session 'that 85 per cent of all brass is supplied to the arms trade?'

The implication of this new piece of information was clear: we should seriously reconsider the ethics of accepting money from a company that made its profits through the arms industry. In fact, it was, I believe, meant to imply that accepting arms industry-related money was in itself unethical.

Ethics is one of the most poorly understood concepts in fundraising, not only in corporate fundraising, but also across the entire spectrum of fundraising techniques. However, many ethical issues are magnified in corporate fundraising because the donors come from a sector of society that has many 'ethical' issues of it own.

But to compound matters, not only is ethics poorly understood; many, if not most, fundraisers believe they have a grasp on corporate fundraising ethics that is not reflected in their actual understanding of the issues.

So this chapter has to start by stating what corporate fundraising ethics is not.

Corporate fundraising ethics is *not*:

- the same as your own personal morality

- dependent on the majority view of fundraisers

- non-evidence-based risk avoidance or minimisation

- non-evidence-based reputation management

- PR

- HR best practice

- fundraising best practice (necessarily, though it can be).

But corporate fundraising ethics *is*:

- a system or code by which you can determine whether you should or should not accept an offer of corporate support that is independent of the factors listed above.

In practice however, many 'ethical' decisions made by corporate fundraisers are actually based on risk avoidance or reputation management or even HR best practice and are not 'ethical' decisions at all. In the worst cases, so-called 'ethical' decisions are based on the personal prejudices of individual fundraisers.

So the starting point for a discussion of corporate fundraising has to be with a discussion of ethical theory itself.

What is ethics?

A broad two-fold definition of ethics is:

1   the philosophical study of the moral value of human conduct and of the rules and principles that ought to govern it
2   a code of conduct considered correct, especially for a professional group.

Ethics in corporate fundraising can therefore be based on whether it is the right thing to do according to the industry's code of practice; or the right thing to do according to a set of higher moral values. But the two may not always conform; in fact sometimes they may conflict.

So as a minimum you, as a corporate fundraiser, have an ethical duty to conform to the Institute of Fundraising's code of practice on corporate fundraising and other relevant codes, especially the code of practice on the acceptance and refusal of donations.

For example, the Institute of Fundraising's code of practice stipulates (paragraph 2.3) that a charity should not work with two companies if this produces a conflict of interest (for example, two companies from the same industry sector). That would be unethical.

But perhaps this not what a lot of fundraisers have in mind when they consider the ethics of corporate fundraising. Rather, they are thinking of ethics according to the first definition – in other words, is it the 'right' thing to do?

According to this scheme, when a donation from a defence firm is turned down, it is because it is the 'right' thing to do (that is, it is 'ethically correct' to refuse donations from companies engaged in the defence industry) not because it conflicts with the IoF Code of Practice.

Ethical theory

So how do you decide the 'right' course of action? There are two broad categories of ethical theory:

Consequentialist (utilitarian). Decide on the right course of action based on what consequences carrying out (or not) that action would have.

Deontological (rights-based). At least partly independent of the consequences of the action. It is the right thing to do according to sets of circumscribed moral rules.

Corporate fundraisers often conflate the two categories and switch between them when making – or more often, retrospectively justifying – their ethical decisions.

A decision to reject a donation from an arms company is often taken on deontological grounds (it is the 'right' thing do to). But when asked to justify that decision, the argument switches to a consequentialist position (it would have a negative effect on public opinion and the charity's reputation and so would have damaged the charity's fundraising in the future).

But consquentialism of this type is actually testable. If you say your donors won't give if you accept this or that corporate partnership, you have a big database that you can segment and ask. If they say they will continue to give, the consequences you fear will not happen, so the consequentialist ethical argument for refusing the donation is undermined.

The consequentialist position is of paramount importance in fundraising because both Charity Commission guidance on the duties of charity trustees and the Institute of Fundraising code of practice on the Acceptance and Refusal of Donations are consequentialist ethical codes.

Charity trustees – and by extension their delegates working for the charity – have a responsibility to always act 'in the best interest of the charity' (Charity Commission guidance, 3). The IoF code of practice says: 'Trustees (or their delegates) have a duty to consider carefully, on the basis of the *evidence* [italics added] available to them, whether the charity's interests will be better serviced by accepting or refusing the donation and to act accordingly.'

The code goes on to say: 'In making judgements, trustees and their authorised decision-maker must not allow individual or collective personal, political or commercial interests, nor personal views on political or ethical issues, which are not directly related to the interests of the charity, to affect their judgement.'

This means that all charities that raise money from companies have an ethical duty to:

- have a clear policy on the acceptance and refusal of donations
- act in the best interest of the charity.

This in turn means basing what is in the charity's best interest on evidence. Corporate fundraisers therefore also have an ethical duty to establish this evidence base through a risk assessment. This could include:

- a PR risk analysis to assess the likelihood of negative media coverage
- surveying a sample of donors to assess their likely giving behaviour were you to accept the donation
- an examination of the company's previous charity partnerships.

It is not enough to say you that you 'think' that partnering such-and-such a company would damage your reputation. That is not evidence; that is gut feeling, which will not suffice to fulfil your responsibilities in establishing evidence.

That is why it is absolutely vital that all corporate fundraising departments have in place robust risk assessment and reputation management procedures that would allow you to conclude, for instance: 'Our research has shown that were we to accept this donation, XX per cent of our current major donors are likely or very likely to withdraw their support, costing us £XXX,000 a year.'

A risk assessment is required under the IoF code of practice on corporate fundraising (paragraph 2.4). I am not sure how many charities actually do conduct such a risk assessment when faced with an ethically problematic corporate partnership.

The consequentialist nature of the Charity Commission guidance and the IoF code of practice all but eliminates the need for a judgement based on deontological grounds.

But let us accept that there is a deontological case for refusing a donation from a company. This position still needs to be justified. If you say it is wrong to accept money from a defence company – then you must say why it is wrong; it is not self-evident. But to say 'because they make weapons and sell them to governments' merely begs the question, because that is just another way to describe what an arms company does. A proper deontological justification could be: 'Because they sell weapons to a regime that uses them to enforce ethnic cleansing.'

But anyone who made a deontological rejection of a corporate donation would then be required to return to the consequentialist position and show why rejecting a donation from a company that was a party to ethnic cleansing was not in the best interest of the charity. In this case, it would be simple: it is not in the best interest of the charity to partner such a company because on deontological grounds genocide is 'wrong', and on consequentialist grounds your reputation would suffer.

But the original argument of 'because they make weapons' is nearly impossible to justify on consequentialist grounds (unless of course there is a specific connection to the charity and its cause), so, in the absence of other reasons, a charity that rejected a donation from an arms company because they *were* an arms company would be acting unethically, not ethically.

Other deontological considerations

Is that it, then? Is all corporate fundraising ethics based on a consequentialist ethical code leaving no room for what is the morally 'correct' choice?

After all, charities are about changing the world so surely there has to be some element of doing the 'right' thing, irrespective of the consequences? Isn't it wrong that you are legally and ethically obliged to accept a donation from a company that you consider to be morally bankrupt? What about that first definition of ethics about judging according to a higher set of human moral values?

Yet the law and the codes of practice are quite clear on this. Decisions must be taken in the best interest of the charity, based on evidence, and not swayed by personal political, commercial or moral preconceptions.

So if you are faced with a corporate partnership that you personally want to refuse on deontological grounds but your professional consequentialist ethical code requires you to accept, who do you resolve this dilemma?

Take some of the considerations in turn.

Knowledge

How much do you know about a company's business practice, ethics or CSR programme – or lack of it? I have used the example of the defence industry throughout this chapter but most companies or industry sectors will have some ethical skeletons in the closet (such as supplier practices, fat cat salaries, environmental footprint, or Third World exploitation).

Suppose you as a corporate fundraiser reject a donation from a company on deontological grounds (or because of your own personal moral position) because, say, you object to the way it 'exploits' workers in the developing world. Then you would also be compelled to reject support from a company that refused to recognise its staff's right to belong to a trade union in the UK, or refused to give them a cost-of-living pay rise. If you didn't, you would leave yourself open to difficult questions about why you are prepared to reject donations from one charity that doesn't treat its workers fairly but accept them from another company that doesn't treat its workers fairly either.

It would be relatively simple to respond to accusations of moral inconsistency if the decisions were taken on consequentialist grounds; less so if the decision were a deontological one.

Your professional ethical code of practice requires you to act based on evidence. So it is beholden on you to find out as much as you possibly can about the company under consideration. It may be ethical to decline a corporate partnership once you have thoroughly researched the issues at hand; it is most definitely not ethical to do so because you heard political comedian Mark Thomas slagging off the company on his TV programme (I once heard a fundraiser cite the Mark Thomas Comedy Product as the source for her information on one controversial company).

Are you an ethicist?

To put it bluntly, what makes you think you are qualified to pronounce on ethical issues? Have you studied philosophy at university? Do you have a layman's grasp of ethical theory? Just because you are a corporate fundraiser doesn't mean you can, or even should, make ethical judgements about corporate fundraising. Take a comparison with the medical professional. A surgeon may be qualified to perform an operation to separate conjoined twins, during which one is certain to die. But this practical ability doesn't qualify him to decide whether or not he *should* carry out this operation.

If you feel you are in a personal/professional moral dichotomy, then begin to resolve it by understanding a little more about the theory and practice of ethics, especially the distinction between consequentialist and deontological codes.

It's not about you – 1

Moral values are not determined by public vote. If there are deontological moral values, they are not arrived at by majority decision. If they were, it would be ethically correct to execute murderers and shoot burglars in this country. All ethical theory recognises this and attempts to separate ethical decision-making from personal opinion.

As we have already seen, the IoF's code on accepting/rejecting donations makes this perfectly clear. Yet there has been talk in the charity sector of canvassing staff opinions on whether or not to accept corporate support.

I hope it is clear that in no way could such a decision be seen as 'ethical'. It may be based on the sum of the personal moral values of its staff, but the final decision would be unethical because:

• there would be no *evidence* that the decision was in the best interest of the charity

• staff would be unlikely to have had sufficient knowledge of the company or of ethical theory to have made an informed choice

• the act would contravene the IoF code of practice on acceptance/ rejection of a donation in that it was swayed by personal opinion.

How do you resolve this quandary? You have three choices:

• resign out of moral principle

• subordinate your personal moral values to your consequentialist code of practice and carry on with your job

• lobby for the charity to change its position or lobby for a change in the codes of practice. We will return to this third option in moment.

Best interest of the charity

What does 'best interest' actually mean? And what constitutes the 'charity' in this regard? Is it the staff, the corporate entity, the cause, the assets, the beneficiaries, or the services it provides?

The law is extremely unsatisfying in this respect. Investigations launched under section 8 of the 1993 Charities Act have tended to safeguard a charity's 'property' (its tangible assets), rather than have regard to its human capital (its beneficiaries, its services and its staff). The 2006 Charities Act leaves this unchanged.

This notwithstanding, the 'best interest of the charity' is vague enough to allow sophisticated argument (or maybe rhetoric?) to justify any course of action – even rejecting a million pounds – as 'in the best interest of the charity'.

But consider this. . .

It's not about you – 2

I believe that, as a fundraiser, your overriding ethical duty is to your beneficiaries. Faced with a difficult ethical choice over an offer of corporate support, what would your beneficiaries want you to do? Would they thank you for refusing £1 million from a defence company?

If you are able, ask them, as this will contribute to your evidence base. Beneficiaries are the most important yet most disenfranchised stakeholders in charities. No one speaks for the beneficiary group in matters such as this.

If you know or you believe that your beneficiary group would want you to accept an offer of support, then if you reject it, you are putting your own personal morality before your duty to your beneficiaries. Should your beneficiaries bear the consequences of your satisfying your own conscience?

This is the third option we touched on above.

Of course, unethical practices can be enshrined in law (slavery for instance), which it is then every ethical person's duty to change. But there are always extremely strong deontological reasons for effecting a change and usually very good consequentialist ones too.

However, as there is nothing to suggest that either Charity Commission guidance or the IoF code of practice on accepting/rejecting donations is ethically unsatisfactory, there are no ethical grounds to lobby for change.

This third option is therefore an ethical non-starter. A corporate fundraiser facing this choice should either resign or subordinate his or her personal morality, but not try to adapt the corporate fundraising environment to accommodate that personal morality.

Professor Hugh La Follette, an ethicist at East Tennessee State University, says: 'We must scrutinise our beliefs, our choices, and our actions to ensure that we a) are sufficiently informed, b) are not unduly swayed by personal interest and c) are not governed by the views of others. Otherwise we may perpetrate evils we could avoid, evils for which future generations will rightly condemn us.'

I will conclude this chapter by adapting that last sentence: Otherwise we may reject donations we should have accepted, actions for which our beneficiaries will rightly condemn us. (See also Appendix Three, page 184, 'An ethical framework for accepting or rejecting corporate support'.)

References

Charities Act 1993 – HMSO
Charities Act 2006 – HMSO
Charity Commission Guidance CC3 – *The Essential Trustee*
Charity Commission Guidance CC20 – *Charities and Fundraising*
Hare, R.M., 'What is wrong with slavery' in Singer, P. *Applied Ethics*, Oxford University Press, 1986
Institute of Fundraising Code of Practice – *The Acceptance and Refusal of Donations*
Institute of Fundraising Code of Practice – *Charities Working with Business*
La Follette, H., *Ethics in Practice*, Blackwell, 1997
Mason, P., 'Don't take the money, and run' in *Professional Fundraising*, mid-June 2004
Markkula Center for Applied Ethics – *A Framework for Thinking Ethically*: www.scu.edu/ethics/practicing/decision/framework.html

Weaver, M., 'Shelter criticised over 'drink for homeless' campaign', *Society Guardian*, 6 October 2004: http://society.guardian.co.uk/homelessness/story/0,8150,1320992, 00.html

PART 2
Case studies from corporate and charity perspectives

CHAPTER EIGHT

Small charity – big success story
A case study from the Foundation for the Study of Infant Deaths

Sara Bowcutt and Catherine Bennett

In today's charity sector, corporate fundraising is big business. It is also a place where big brand charities often rule. Ask anyone and they can name a brand that has 'gone pink', or a company working with a major charity. Most people, whether you are a third-sector employee or member of the public, could name a big UK charity. The fact that some UK charities are now some the most recognised brands in the country is testament to the power of their cause in today's society and the commercial power big charities like this possess.

However, there is definitely a place for smaller charities in corporate fundraising. The challenge is for them to know how to get started and to be able to compete. How should they convince big companies that there are benefits to be had from working with them? At the Foundation for the Study of Infant Deaths we use our relatively small size to our advantage. We realise our value to companies and use this in our corporate fundraising strategy. We also promote our flexibility as a reason to work with us over larger charities and make sure companies know the huge impact their support can have. We feel that because of this we have a number of successful corporate partners.

The smaller charity perspective

The Foundation for the Study of Infant Deaths (FSID) is the UK's leading baby charity working to prevent sudden infant death and promote baby health and safety. We offer support to bereaved families through a number of national services. We spread lifesaving messages on how to reduce the risk of sudden infant death through the distribution of information leaflets, working with the media and with health care professionals, and through other means. All of our advice is informed by research into the causes and risk factors of infant death. Our funded research is world class and has enabled us to advise parents and professionals on how to reduce the risk of cot death and since our inception there has been a significant reduction in cot death rates – nearly 75 per cent. This is an achievement of which we are extremely proud.

In terms of structure we are a relatively small charity. We have 13 full-time and 13 part-time members of staff, and we also rely on a number of regular and dedicated volunteers. We are almost entirely dependent on donations and our annual income from companies, trusts, individuals and events is around £1.3 million per annum.

We may be small but our CV speaks for itself. Not only have we worked in partnership with large companies but we are also seen as the experts in our field. We work with government and other policy-makers, and many thousands of health professionals have come to us for advice. This adds weight to our corporate partnerships through the benefits we can offer them by giving them access to these markets.

We have a strong history of corporate fundraising. Corporate-related marketing (CRM) has been a particularly successful area for us, as has corporate sponsorship of our information resources for parents and health professionals. We have worked with big companies like Babies R Us, Mothercare and Ikea on highly successful CRM promotions which have raised substantial funds for FSID. Corporate sponsors over the years have included Boots, Johnson & Johnson, Tomy and Next. These are well known and big name companies, all of whom saw the value of working with us despite our size.

FSID's corporate fundraising strategy

Our corporate fundraising strategy is based on the fact that we are a smaller charity but one that has made a big impact on our cause. We are realistic in our approach but also innovative in our corporate work.

We want to increase our presence within the corporate sector but understand this is a long process. Therefore we have built up a four-year plan of how to achieve this, ensuring we increase our targets and outputs each year in line with our strategy. We aim to make use of all corporate fundraising mechanisms: CRM, appropriate charity of the year, sponsorship, philanthropic mailings, corporate trusts and foundations, gifts in kind. We also emphasise donor care, something that as a smaller charity we can really excel at. But we are always realistic. Like all corporate fundraising teams, we have an extensively researched charity of the year calendar but we only apply for those for which we could, at this point, provide the resources those partnerships demand. We concentrate on the smaller, but equally important, adoptions on which we know we can deliver.

We also ensure that there is room and time for innovation. We are not afraid to try new things and test new ideas. Sometimes we fail and other times our innovation and flexibility really work. Our relationship with gro-group® is an example of our success in this area.

The case study

gro-group® is a nursery products distributor, and is best known for its multi-award-winning grobag® baby sleeping bag, a 'wearable' blanket that is designed as a safe alternative to traditional sheets and blankets. When grobag® baby sleeping bags were launched in September 2000, the concept of baby sleeping bags was almost unknown in the UK. Today, gro-group® is the UK's market leader in baby sleeping bags.

From the beginning of gro-group®'s idea for a UK baby sleeping bag, FSID was involved. gro-group® wanted to work to ensure that their products created a safe sleeping environment for babies, so they approached FSID.

We were able to share with them our vast research on safer sleeping environments for babies. At the same time, we were looking to build awareness of our advice for parents on how to reduce the risk of cot death and were looking for corporate partners to increase our funding. It soon became apparent that our similar objectives could be leveraged if we worked more closely together.

The opportunity for grobag® to help educate consumers with our safer sleep advice was and still is key to our relationship. Together we looked for opportunities on product packaging, advertising and promotional literature to promote our advice. Each grobag® comes with a free nursery thermometer, which helps parents monitor room temperature (an important aspect of baby safety). The thermometer has FSID's 'reduce the risk' messages on the back. These messages have now been seen on over one million grobag® products and are a vital way for us to reach parents and for grobag® to be linked to the safe infant care message.

The values we share are fundamental to the grobag® business proposition and always have been. This is an essential part of successfully undertaking corporate partnerships and if the charity is small, to ensure that partnerships don't become one sided.

A key aspect of the product launch plan was to provide credible research and information as backing for their baby sleeping bag product. The input of FSID was vital to this. Gro-group® sees the importance of FSID's involvement; we are partners and this makes our relationship very special.

The objective for gro-group® at the time of the product launch was to gain trust from consumers and health professionals that their baby sleeping bag product was safe, and to encourage parents to try baby sleeping bags as a safe alternative to traditional bedding.

When the relationship was initially established, we ensured that our board of trustees understood the ethos of gro-group® and their new product. There is buy-in at every level of the organisation for this relationship; another important aspect of successful corporate partnerships.

Our relationship with gro-group® is constantly developing and we are always on the lookout for different ways of working together and exploring new product development. The grobag® egg™, a colour-changing digital room thermometer is a new product we are currently working on together.

FSID and gro-group® are now fully committed to a five-year partnership which will see FSID benefit from substantial funding and ensure our safety messages reach parents across the country. For gro-group®, our expertise means the sleeping bags are seen as a trusted baby product, so much so that in 2006 they were given the status of 'Kids Superbrand' (www.superbrands.org.uk).

Marketing magic

The partnership we have with gro-group® is fundamental to their marketing plan and FSID's 'reduce the risk' messages appear on packaging for both baby sleeping bags and the grobag® egg. The FSID logo and 'reduce the risk' messages have also appeared on the majority of grobag® advertising since their launch. This equates to an estimated eight million OTSs (opportunities to see).

The success of the partnership lies in the fact that it is so important for both parties. The income we receive from gro-group® is currently unmatched by any other corporate partner and our messages are received by millions of parents. For gro-group®, as a result of the partnership, they are able to work with the expert in baby health and safety and have seen a rise in sales, making them the leading manufacturer of baby sleeping bags in the country.

> 'We believe our relationship with FSID strengthens our market position and adds credibility to our reputation and our products. We are extremely happy that our partnership has gone from strength to strength and looks set to continue'.
>
> Rob Holmes, grobag® founder

The management process

Both FSID and gro-group® have gained valuable and measurable benefits from the partnership, a true testament to company/charity working. It also highlights just how valuable small charities can be to companies.

Our long-standing relationship means we have clear and open lines of communication at all times. There is one main account manager but other members of staff from both organisations are in regular contact. We are constantly evaluating the impact our partnership has, be that in terms of sales, media interest or awareness raising. Through regular personal updates and face-to-face meetings we ensure any issues, good or bad, are dealt with quickly and successfully.

It was recognised from the outset that having a common goal could add a great deal of value to the partnership, not least in being able to support each other's wider objectives.

Successes so far

In terms of brand recognition we have both been successful in increasing our brand awareness. grobag® created a new baby bedding category in the UK, and its success as a new brand and product has been enhanced due to the credibility offered by the association with FSID, and the reassurance that this offers the consumer.

grobag® has won many awards, such as Tommy's Parent Friendly Awards, and *Mother & Baby Magazine* Gold Award for Best Nursery Item two years running as well as being named a Kids Superbrand. It has gone from a new company to a market leader in a few short years while FSID's advice has reached a whole new group of parents and been mentioned in countless press releases and media articles.

Our mandate to inform and educate the public is greatly supported by our partnership and increases awareness of our safe sleep messages. We believe that our partnership offers gro-group® a competitive advantage in the baby products market and ensures our messages stay in the public consciousness.

gro-group® has also benefited from access to new audiences. The partnership has paved the way for the grobag® brand to be more accessible to midwives and health visitors, a group known to be resistant to pro-moting commercial messages. Through working with FSID, gro-group® was able to access every maternity unit and primary care trust in the country and achieve branding on 150,000 cot stickers, each of which promoted our 'reduce the risk of cot death' messages. These stickers were distributed to midwives and health visitors with whom they were very popular. This campaign was highly successful in promoting our messages and gro-group® were able to access a new audience.

Perhaps the biggest benefit for the company is the positive effect our partnership has on sales. Thirty-three percent of parents now use baby sleeping bags instead of traditional sheets and blankets, with grobag® having a third of the market share (Independent Market Research, July 2004). It is estimated that the company now sells one grobag® baby sleeping bag every 60 seconds.

gro-group® are not the only ones who benefit from this partnership. FSID's lifesaving messages are also promoted. This promotional work has led to an estimated 13.5 million OTSs over the last five years. We also believe that the continual publicity of FSID on grobag® products and promotional literature has kept awareness of FSID on the agenda amongst independent nursery retailers and parents. To a charity, can anything be more important than spreading the message?

Of course, we benefit in a financial way too, and the financial support we receive from gro-group® is substantial and in line with the credibility and benefits we afford them. As mentioned earlier, we know our value as do gro-group® and this is reflected in the financial contributions we receive from them.

All of the successes of our partnership so far have been achieved through working closely in partnership, through communicating clearly and through understanding each other's commercial and charitable aims.

Key learning points

Our relationship has come a long way since its inception and we have learned a number of important lessons during this time. Each of these lessons enables us to continue to have a successful partnership and can be applied to other corporate relationships at FSID and other charities.

Here is what we have learned:

1. Ensure that you have a system of open, honest communication. It is imperative that you have a relationship with your corporate partner that enables you to discuss things openly and frankly, whether positive or negative.
2. Ensure that there is always a commercial agreement in place and that specifics and responsibilities have been agreed before any campaign or partnership begins. This will help ensure that gremlins don't crop up unannounced once the partnership has been launched.
3. Flexibility is key as problems will come up. The key is to be able to deal with these in a flexible manner and through open discussion. In addition, don't be afraid to compromise as long as this is something that both the charity and corporate partner undertake and that it will help to ensure that things can move forward.

4. Ensure that there are experienced staff in place. You will need experienced staff within the charity that are dedicated to looking after your corporate partnerships and are able to negotiate effectively.
5. Build in extra time! You always need more time than you think, so always build in a good few weeks in order to ensure there is enough time to finish things properly without having to rush.
6. Remember the importance of development and innovation. Always think of ways to develop your corporate relationships. Don't be afraid to innovate and try new things. It will bring a freshness to your relationship and will open new avenues
7. Know the value of your brand. All charity brands are valuable to companies; it is why they want to work with charities. Be aware of this and don't be afraid to stand firm on issues of charity practice and principle. As long as you always remember the importance of being flexible, you will be more respected for doing so.

Future plans

As corporate fundraisers, we are always looking for long-term strategic partnerships and there is a reason for that. They give us more time to develop, to grow, and to see real benefits from our partnerships. That is what our relationship with gro-group® is: real partnership working. And we intend it to stay that way. We see this as an ongoing partnership and hope that it continues to develop.

New product development such as the grobag® egg highlights that this can be achieved. gro-group® is also given the opportunity to support other events and publications and we hope that in the future this will happen more often, giving extra weight to our relationship.

We also hope to undertake further CRM promotions and this is an area that both FSID and gro-group® are constantly exploring and discussing, keeping lines of communication firmly open.

The benefits both FSID and gro-group® have reaped from our relationship so far mean there is a very strong foundation for us to continue working in partnership and both parties continue to look for ways to develop.

Conclusion

At first glance, FSID could appear to be a smaller charity with little to offer large corporate partners. We operate in a specialist area and could be viewed as too niche to offer benefits to a wide audience. But our partnership with gro-group® highlights that small charities can offer real and substantial benefits to companies and reap significant financial gains for themselves.

It also shows that small charities can compete in today's corporate sector if they follow a few basic rules. Perhaps most importantly they should know their worth. FSID is proud of its reputation as an expert in the field of baby health and this is something we are unwilling to compromise on. This reputation means that we have standing within the public eye and this gives us great commercial power, power that companies want to tap into. Many small charities will have the same power; they just might not take advantage of it.

Though we are confident about the benefits we can offer, we are also realistic about what we can achieve and this too is an important part of success in the corporate sector. We also put an emphasis on *partnership* working: working together to achieve a common goal and being equals in the relationship.

We believe that our innovation coupled with these areas is key to our successful corporate partnerships. Our partnership with gro-group® highlights the fact that small charities can compete with big ones when it comes to corporate fundraising. We can be successful in these partnerships, we just need to believe we can be and go out there and get it!

CHAPTER NINE

EDF Energy – managing our impacts on the community

Alison Braybrooks

The latest research conducted by Ipsos Mori in September 2006 shows how important the issue of corporate responsibility is to all customer-led businesses. An overwhelming majority of the public wants businesses to consider how their activities affect society and the environment and, crucially, 83 per cent state that a company's social responsibility is an important consideration when they are purchasing a product or service.

These findings are particularly relevant to a company such as EDF Energy, one of the largest energy companies in the UK. While we at EDF Energy believe that our business is fundamentally beneficial to society, we also recognise that our operations have the potential to impact negatively on the community. This makes an effective community programme a business imperative.

In devising our community programme, we involved stakeholders across the company as well as from our diverse customer base and the community. We challenged them to identify the key impacts – both positive and negative – that EDF Energy's activities have on local communities.

We were able to distil all the identified impacts into three key cross-company impact areas:

- environment (including climate change and biodiversity)
- vulnerable and fuel poor customers
- safety

and from this we defined our vision for the community.

'We provide an essential service to millions of customers, and are therefore integral to the communities we serve. We believe that we have a responsibility to provide this service in a way that is accessible and affordable for our vulnerable customers, safe for the whole community, while minimising the impact on the environment. The community programme supports our responsible business practice in achieving this.

'Our people are central to this. We encourage all of them to get involved in our local communities and support them with time and funding. As a result, thousands of them each year help us to build healthy, sustainable communities.'

EDF Energy vision for the community

So, how did we go about developing our programme? This chapter explores the processes that EDF Energy went through to get to our community vision. This is followed by a discussion of the programme that we have chosen to deliver on our vision. Finally, how the programme is managed is considered, and how its results are evaluated.

Developing the programme

Business in the Community (BiTC) publishes a guide to corporate community investment, which helped us to develop our own community investment (CI) model. Using this model ensures that we have a balanced approach that manages our impacts, meets the needs of our stakeholders and helps us to achieve our ambitions as a business. (You can find more information on developing a community programme on BiTC's website BiTC.org.uk)

FIGURE 9.1 DEVELOPING THE COMMUNITY INVESTMENT MODEL

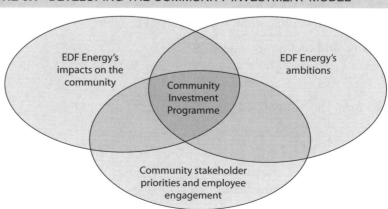

It is worth understanding in detail each of the key areas of our CI model.

EDF Energy's ambitions

EDF Energy has the ambition to be a passionate, committed, caring, innovative, and successful energy company enabling our people to make a difference.

As a way of achieving this ambition we have developed five subsidiary ambitions, each of which relates to one or more of our stakeholders. The subsidiary ambition that guides our community programme is:

'We want to be a safe and responsible company regarding our people, the environment and the communities we serve.'

We have set ourselves a challenging strategic target for this ambition, which is to rank top among our peers in a recognised corporate responsibility (CR) index. We have chosen the Business in the Community annual CR index as our benchmark.

So, in order to meet our ambitions as a business, our community programme must fit within our overall CR strategy, match current best practice by helping us to manage our impacts and ensure that we involve our stakeholders in its design.

Stakeholder priorities and employee engagement

Using our CI model, the next step was to find out what areas our stakeholders thought we should focus on.

First, we undertook a company-wide consultation, which included workshops, an intranet survey, and meetings with key managers responsible for areas of the business that impacted on the community. The key focus areas that emerged here were climate change and energy efficiency.

Next, we fed in results from our ongoing consultation with customers on issues that affect them or are of concern to them. The environment figured particularly highly as an issue for our customers.

Crucially, we also consulted with some of our existing and new community partners, including Business in the Community, and the London Benchmarking Group. We asked for their views on what our key priorities for the community should be. The answers focused on the company's support for vulnerable customers as well as, again, the environment.

Community impacts

All business areas in EDF Energy carry out an annual risk assessment, covering all aspects of their operations. This information is collated centrally by the Risk Team, providing an excellent source to understand the company's impacts on the community.

Here is an overview of our detailed study, with impacts identified for each business activity:

FIGURE 9.2 COMMUNITY IMPACT OF BUSINESS ACTIVITIES

Business activity	Community impact
Coal and gas fired power stations	CO_2 – contributing to climate change Sulphur emissions – contributing to poor air quality and acid rain
Network distribution areas	High-voltage network sites – creating a potential danger to the public CO_2 emissions from transport – contributing to climate change Significant land ownership – opportunities for promoting biodiversity
EDF Energy (supply business)	Vulnerable customers – creating a need to support them so that they can access our services Fuel poor customers – creating a need to help our customers manage their fuel bills and overall debt Energy efficiency – a need to educate and incentivise energy efficiency
Major office locations	CO_2 emissions – contributing to climate change
CHP (combined heat and power) and wind farms	Physical presence – impact on the visual environment

We felt that a small number of 'impact groups' would be the best way to manage these impacts within the community programme. Three groups naturally emerged that accounted for our key community impacts: environment; vulnerable and fuel poor customers; and safety.

The community investment (CI) programme

These three key elements – company ambitions, community impacts and stakeholder engagement – together underpin EDF Energy's community programme.

The activities are grouped by impact area.

Environment

We are keen to establish a true competitive point of difference by placing long-term sustainability at the heart of our business agenda – a unique approach in the energy sector.

We have developed a range of business activities that tackle our impact on the environment right across the company:

• setting tough targets to increase the amount of electricity we generate from renewable sources, and reduce carbon emissions

• investing over £200 million in flue gas desulphurisation in our power stations to improve air quality

• signing up to the Energy Saving Trust Transport Charter – a 20 per cent CO_2 reduction in transport emissions

• launching 'read/reduce/reward', a ground-breaking customer programme where we reward customers for reducing their consumption year on year

• investing substantially in improving energy efficiency for our customers in their homes

• improving our day-to-day activities in offices championed by One Planet ambassadors, for example, recycling and energy use

• producing biodiversity action plans for each major site.

The community programme supports this by building partnerships with national organisations to support our activities with expert advice and opportunities to involve employees.

One example is the Wildlife Trusts, which we have joined as top-level members in all our areas of operation. We already had a long-standing partnership with them in East Anglia and at our Doxford office (in Sunderland), but we have now formalised this partnership right across the business. We are working with the Wildlife Trusts to develop biodiversity action plans for our major sites. Our One Community ambassadors (see 'Employee involvement', below) are also working with them locally to organise volunteering activities at local Trust reserves, offering both practical and management support.

Vulnerable and fuel poor customers

The government definition of fuel poverty is when a household has to spend over 10 per cent of its post-tax income on heating. Tackling fuel poverty is one of our most important social responsibilities, and we have developed a sector-leading response:

• Using innovative modelling techniques, we have identified our fuel poor customers and targeted them with a number of initiatives from a low-cost tariff, debt assistance to free installation of energy efficiency measures in their homes.

• Across our London Warm Zone we are working with a range of partners to improve housing quality, and to help our customers access government benefits, and reduce their energy bills.

• We give customers who are having trouble paying their bills help and advice through a free pack that provides them with information on a variety of payment options, energy efficiency advice and available grants, other helplines and relevant organisations, and useful tools to aid their budget planning.

The community programme supports this activity by engaging with community stakeholders who have broad experience of dealing with vulnerable and fuel poor customers. We deal with customers from the perspective of their energy consumption, but vulnerable and fuel poor customers often face a whole range of challenges. By understanding their situation better, we can tailor our approach to ensure that we are providing excellent service to all our customers.

We have developed two major partnerships aimed at fuel poor and vulnerable customers.

The first is Citizens Advice, the leading advice organisation in the UK, dealing with over 5 million problems every year through a network of bureaux. Through our grant programme, we have funded £750,000 for debt advisors in Citizens Advice Bureaux in areas where we know there are fuel poor customers. Our One Community ambassadors are also building relationships with bureaux close to our offices and are supporting them with volunteering and management advice. We are also working with them on national policy regarding fuel poverty.

Our second major partnership is with Mencap, which is also our national charity fundraising partner. We aimed to raise £100,000 for Mencap matched with £100,000 of company funding in our first year, and have so far raised almost £500,000 (including matching) in two years of partnership. We organise quarterly national events, including an annual flagship event, and our One Community ambassadors run a whole range of local site events in between.

Perhaps even more importantly, we work with Mencap on improving our billing, using their expertise to make our communications more accessible to people with a learning disability. We are also piloting Workright, where we are offering employment to people with a learning disability at our key sites.

Safety

We have a Public Safety Manager, responsible for working with the community to highlight the dangers of electricity and to devise strategies for protecting the public.

Our community programme to support this is Power-up, our comprehensive schools programme, covering all our areas of network operation, reaching 300,000 school children every year with safety advice both outside and in the home and working in partnership with Junior Citizen and Crucial Crew to deliver safety messages at their events

Employee involvement

Our employees are central to our community activity, so it is vital that any programme maximises their involvement. We have a number of initiatives that motivate and enable our employees to get involved in the community.

The company's main vehicle for employee engagement is Helping Hands. This has been running for six years. In Helping Hands, we give each of our employees two days' paid work time to volunteer in the community. In 2005, 2,710 employees (around 15 per cent) took part in this, making Helping Hands one of the largest company-supported volunteering programmes in the UK.

Building on the success of Helping Hands, and to strengthen our volunteering activity, we have launched an Ambassador programme. This has further embedded our community activity right across the business. We have recruited over 200 One Community ambassadors, from every site. Their role is to champion fundraising and environmental activity locally and to enthuse their colleagues to get involved. They are given an enhanced Helping Hands allowance of two hours per week and work with our national community partners – such as Mencap, the Citizens' Advice Bureaux and the Wildlife Trusts – on a local basis.

Another element of our programme is matched giving. We know that many of our employees have their own favourite charities or local community projects, and EDF Energy matches up to £100 raised per employee per year. For Mencap, the employees' chosen national charity, we match pound for pound with no individual employee limit.

Our employees were instrumental in the selection of Mencap as the chosen charity. We offered our employees the chance to choose a charity 'theme' from a range linked to the key impact areas. They chose 'health and disability', related to the Fuel Poor and Vulnerable Customers impact area. We then asked four charities from this area to present to a cross-company committee, led by the Director of Communications and the Chief Operating Officer for Customers Branch, which resulted in the selection of Mencap. Mencap offered the best fit in terms of our joint objectives for vulnerable people and also gave a fantastic and challenging presentation led by their chief executive.

Managing the programme

Our director of communications is responsible for representing community issues in the company's executive committee discussions, supported by a new Community Investment Strategy Group made up of representatives from all parts of the business.

The purpose of this group is to ensure that community investment is embedded into our responsible business practice throughout the business.

The group is supported by a central CI team and a network of corporate responsibility managers across the business. The CR managers meet regularly with our sponsorship and marketing managers to agree how the strategy set by the CI strategy group can be translated into action across the business, and to ensure that it fits with our community-focused marketing and branding activities.

Communications with community partners

We meet with our community partners quarterly to assess progress against annual objectives and to forward plan.

For our key partners such as Mencap, the communication process is more rigorous. We have an annual planning meeting between Mencap and the original selection panel, where we review progress against our original objectives for the partnership and set new ones. The community investment team and local corporate responsibility managers then meet the Mencap team every month to review progress and plan. The Mencap team contact the One Community ambassadors monthly to support them in their local fundraising. They also visit each major site across the partnership, to meet the fundraising team, and also to talk to employees about the issues facing people with a learning disability.

For our major fundraising initiatives we put together a project plan, with tasks allocated for the Mencap and EDF Energy teams, and hold a weekly conference call in the run-up to the event to check on progress.

Evaluation

We use three methods of external evaluation to benchmark our activities and to improve and grow our programme.

The London Benchmarking Group (LBG) Index measures our community investment spend and the impact of our programme on the community. We also work closely with LBG throughout the year to help us devise our programme. They are very good at asking the hard questions on whether our ideas would develop the right sort of impacts.

The CR Index operated by BiTC, benchmarks us against over 150 other companies (including almost all companies in our sector) to ensure that we are meeting best practice in all areas of corporate responsibility. This is a very high-profile list, featured in the *Sunday Times* and the *Financial Times* and a high place is one of our key ambitions as a business. In the 2006 Index we were ranked equal 29th.

Finally, we have just introduced a stakeholder panel to formalise our relationships with key stakeholders, and to ensure we are meeting their priorities.

Conclusion

We take our responsibilities to the community very seriously. We believe the community programme should support responsible business practice, and enable our employees to get involved.

'We are aligning our community programme with our business activity and using it as a great way to engage employees and make them feel good about their company. It is also a powerful way to build positive relationships with people living in the communities where we work and who are affected by what we do.'

Gareth Wynn, EDF Energy Director of Communications, Executive Responsibility for Community

CHAPTER TEN

Brand synergy on the beach
A case study from RNLI and Wall's

Philippa Thompson

The RNLI is a registered charity that saves lives at sea. We provide a 24 hour on-call service to cover search and rescue requirements out to 100 nautical miles from the coast of the UK and Republic of Ireland, and a seasonal beach lifeguard service on beaches in the south-west of England, which is set to expand nationally. We are independent from the government and rely on the public and business sectors' generosity to support the RNLI's vital work.

Every year around 100 people drown on or around UK beaches and a further 7,000 people get into serious difficulties. In 2005, RNLI lifeguards attended 8,644 incidents during the summer season. With more people than ever before using the sea and beach, the demands placed on RNLI crews and lifeguards have never been greater.

Statistics indicate that beach safety education is having an impact on the reduction of serious incidents. The RNLI's beach safety programme aims to save lives through educating beach users and raising safety awareness. Preventing accidents before they happen is 90 per cent of a lifeguard's job.

Background to the partnership between the RNLI and Wall's

Wall's has a major share of the ice-cream market with the majority of their sales coming from the impulse range: the highest in the industry. The impulse range is a Wall's success story and includes brands like Magnum, Solero and Cornetto. The kids range is specially formulated for young tastebuds, and shows an understanding of children's nutritional needs.

With unrivalled success in the impulse ice-cream market, which is strongly linked to holidaying and days out at the beach, Wall's recognise that it has a responsibility for promoting safety in communities where they have the greatest market share. The RNLI is committed to saving lives at sea, and we invest in safety education programmes for children and their families in order to prevent accidents on the beaches and coastal waters of the UK. The south-west of England is the most visited beach destination in the UK and it was no coincidence that both Wall's and the RNLI originally focused safety efforts in this area.

While a partnership between Birds Eye Fish Fingers and RNLI can be traced back to one of the very first cause-related marketing initiatives in 1969, our relationship with Wall's began in 2004. At this point our beach safety and education teams were working with Wall's to raise awareness about potential dangers on the beach through a wristband campaign managed by a third party company. The Child Safe Campaign was relatively small scale but it reached thousands of children and their families, and importantly it was an opportunity for Wall's to experience our professionalism and reach on the beaches.

In 2004, both Wall's and the RNLI were working on programmes alongside the Child Safe Campaign. Wall's was providing safety information through their award winning Wall's Waterwise safety roadshow, and we were recognised as the lead provider of water and beach safety and education through our own roadshow and school-based work.

Wall's wanted to further develop and invest in education and water safety to help fulfil their CSR objectives, but their roadshow was duplicating work we were already carrying out. They recognised that if they joined forces with us they would have access to a stronger programme, and the added benefit of aligning with our highly valued brand. Wall's terminated their own Wall's Waterwise programme and approached us in April 2005 to form a partnership for that summer. We only had a month to pitch for, and discuss, the terms of sponsorship before rollout; it was a challenging but exciting prospect!

We realised that, in order to secure the partnership, we needed to be clear about what we had already planned, our objectives, how Wall's could strengthen the activities, and how they could align their brand in a meaningful way. The key was to be flexible, to react where possible to Wall's timescales, and to present sponsorship opportunities that would ensure a smooth transition from their own programme.

From the initial discussions it was clear that Wall's' objectives were in line with our own. Taking into account the short timescale, a proposal was put together highlighting the possible sponsorship elements of our established beach safety projects including: Beach To City, a beach safety project for children in Birmingham (identified as high-risk beach users); the beach safety roadshow; Shorething, our education website; an aerial beach safety banner campaign; beach safety publications; the *Sea Safe* magazine for children; and Concertina SAFE, a small leaflet containing key safety messages used as a give-away at events throughout the UK and Republic of Ireland.

Wall's objectives

- get water/beach safety messages into schools

- educate children up to the age of 18 years old on these messages

- run a national campaign

- have a long-term partnership with a reputable organisation that will help deliver the safety messages effectively

The RNLI education and Beach Safety objectives

- save lives at sea by changing attitudes and behaviours

- be the leading provider of sea safety information to 4–18 year olds

- educate, engage and involve young people in sea safety and the role of the RNLI as a charity by:

  - providing effective and engaging sea safety resources
  - encouraging safer behaviour
  - encouraging active involvement with the RNLI
  - encouraging fundraising

Pilot stage – using the systems already in place to deliver a shared message

Wall's wanted to replace like with like, so funding the beach safety road-show was the obvious choice. They also wanted to achieve a national reach and sponsoring the beach safety publications gave them this opportunity. Through these two projects Wall's were able to align themselves with the core activities of the RNLI's beach safety programme, and achieve a localised and national reach. In sponsoring similar activities to those that they had run in previous years, they were able to maintain consistent messages in the community and enhance them through the highly visual partnership of a well-loved and respected national charity.

Our Lifeguards and Wall's brands are well matched; both use bright red and yellow colours to represent brands that are well loved, respected and child focused, and strongly linked to the summer, safety and fun. Visual branding opportunities offered to Wall's in return for their 2005 sponsorship included logos on the outside and inside of the beach safety trailer, and on all the beach safety publications.

Beach Safety roadshow

Overview: A 16ft roadshow, towed by a branded 4 × 4 vehicle with seasonal driver. In 2005 the roadshow visited approximately 50 events and reached over 10,000 children mainly in the south, at school visits, youth organisations, beaches, key events and life skills centres. The roadshow included: a plasma screen, PA equipment, rescue boat, rescue jet ski and other lifeguard equipment to provide a visually engaging and hard-hitting way to communicate the safety messages to young people.

Timescale: On tour from May to October each summer.

Benefits: Wall's branding on the trailer, roadshow and driver.

Beach Safety publications

Overview: Various safety publications including leaflets and fliers aimed at a wide target audience. Publications are distributed nationally at Tourist Information, hotels, tourist attractions and on the beaches. In addition posters, tattoos, T-shirts and stickers are given away at key events.

Timescale: Distributed May to October.

Benefits: Wall's branding on all the publications.

Pilot programme results – impact on the beaches/in RNLI/in Wall's

In 2005, over 10,000 children visited the roadshow and learnt how to keep themselves safe on the beach. Safety messages were also delivered through 175,000 Wall's-sponsored beach safety publications that were distributed to key locations such as Little Chefs, service stations en route to the sea, hotel chains and tourist attractions. One of the key beach safety messages is understanding what the beach flags mean:

• **Red-and-yellow flags** mark the areas of water that are patrolled by lifeguards. This is the safest area to swim.

• **Black-and-white chequered flags** are marked out for use by craft (such as windsurfers, kayaks). It is not safe to swim in this area.

• The **red flag** flying alone signifies danger.

At the end of the summer of 2005, an independent research company interviewed over 1,000 people on three beaches in the South West of England and found an increase in awareness on the previous year for:

- understanding what the red-and-yellow flags mean (up 9% to 63%)

- understanding what the black-and-white flags mean (up 3% to 31%)

- understanding what the red flags mean (up 3% to 91%).

While we were able to meet Wall's' objectives in 2005 we realised we were in a vulnerable position as sponsorship had only been agreed for one year. The partnership needed to be strategically developed so Wall's could see the value of making a long-term investment. By aligning them to a core element of the beach safety programme it was guaranteed that we would prove ourselves on programme delivery, but in order to establish ourselves as a longer-term partner we needed to engage Wall's with our cause, and demonstrate our professionalism in managing the relationship.

In order to achieve this, Wall's were firstly introduced to a dedicated point of contact within the RNLI's corporate fundraising team. A fortunate coincidence was that at the same time the Beach Fundraising Manager became a Corporate Fundraising Manager, and was best placed to coordinate the RNLI publications, operations (Beach Safety), regional and divisional education teams' input into the Wall's-sponsored project.

Second, the Corporate Fundraising Manager brought Wall's closer to RNLI's work by communicating the scope of the Lifeguards and beach safety programme, and the impact that Wall's sponsorship was having on child safety. Wall's were also invited to key RNLI events, and wherever possible these events were used as sampling opportunities for their products.

Developing the partnership – mutual benefit

On the back of the success of the 2005 summer season, we met with Wall's to review activities, present the results of the independent research, and discuss the opportunities for further sponsorship. Within the RNLI the beach safety programme was proving its value at preventing accidents, and attracting high-profile corporate support. The programme also met our organisational objectives of reaching a younger, broader segment of the population and presenting our work in a relevant and dynamic way.

Wall's were keen to extend their support in 2006 and move to a more child-focused safety programme. We saw this is as an opportunity to integrate their brand more fully, and upgrade the level of financial support. Wall's chose to continue funding the beach safety roadshow, and to take up sponsorship of the Hit the Surf programme. Hit the Surf is a surf-lifesaving course available to children aged 8–12 years old which takes place on the beach and in the water; local schoolchildren have the opportunity to learn from the RNLI Lifeguards about surfing safety, lifesaving and the dangers around the beach in a real, but safe, environment.

The shift from a national reach to a more child-focused approach meant that Wall's chose not to sponsor the beach safety publications. However, the total value of the sponsorship in 2006 represented a 36 per cent increase on 2005.

In 2006 our beach safety programme built on the achievements of the previous year, and over 15,000 children received beach safety messages through the touring road show, school visits, and the Hit the Surf programme. Awareness of the beach safety flags and the role of the Lifeguards was also up, all of which led to a real-terms reduction in accidents.

Successes to date

Our partnership with Wall's has been a success on many fronts. First, funding from Wall's has enabled us to expand our beach safety programme delivering vital safety messages to thousands of children and families. Second, the Lifeguards and Beach Safety team are proud to be aligned with such a high-profile brand, and the Wall's sponsorship has strengthened the perception of the fledgling Lifeguards programme.

Wall's know they can depend on us to maintain the integrity of their brand and add value through our own position as a much-loved and respected national institution. They are also confident that we have the expertise and resources to deliver a strong, goal-driven programme.

The relationship between Wall's and the RNLI has been built on mutual respect. We are both clear on what each party is bringing to the partnership and there are defined lines of communication. Internally, the Corporate Fundraising Department has developed an excellent working relationship with the departments delivering the beach safety programme. Clear communication within the organisation has ensured that Wall's' expectations are understood by everyone involved in delivering the programme and they can respond by sharing news directly relating to Wall's' investment.

This joint venture supports what many corporate fundraisers already believe – that as long as a partnership is built on mutually beneficial terms and remains creative and relevant, it is easier to upgrade an established corporate supporter than to search out and pitch for new support.

Challenges to date

An initial challenge was the short turnaround time to pitch for and deliver the project. However, we assured the quality of the partnership by aligning Wall's with already tried and tested projects.

A more sensitive issue has been the need to negotiate the partnership year on year. From an implementation angle this makes financial planning for the beach education programmes less efficient and more vulnerable. It also means any new projects that Wall's are keen to sponsor have to be rushed through. From a departmental viewpoint, it means we don't have the flexibility to establish a long-term vision for our brand alignments.

The future of the partnership

The brand values shared between the RNLI and Wall's offer many opportunities for expansion. In order for the partnership to expand and continue to meet both organisation's objectives, we would like to move to a stage when we can rely on Wall's to fund core elements of the beach safety programme and we can add value to their sponsorship. This could include addressing wider objectives within their CSR policy, developing training and volunteering opportunities for Wall's' staff based around a lifeguarding theme, and sharing communications from the programme more widely within the organisation.

A currently untapped area is directly linking the programme to Wall's products. For example, a cause-related marketing initiative with one of the Wall's ice creams, including a wrapper safety message, would target tens of thousands more children, strengthen Wall's' position as the number one caring ice-cream brand, and raise more money for our beach safety programme. With the proposed expansion of the Lifeguards programme in 2007/08, more opportunities for collaboration will present themselves. As long as the partnership continues to be creative and forward thinking, we hope that we can work with Wall's to prevent tragic accidents on the UK's beaches.

CHAPTER ELEVEN

Integrating corporate fundraising into an overall fundraising strategy
A case study of TreeHouse

Susan Beck

This chapter explores how the charity TreeHouse has integrated corporate fundraising into an overall fundraising strategy to benefit all income streams. It explains how TreeHouse uses the relationships built through corporate fundraising to open doors to other income streams including trusts, individuals and community supporters and similarly utilises its ongoing fundraising programme to access corporate support.

Context

Background to TreeHouse

Founded in 1997, TreeHouse is the national charity for autism education. It aims to address a dire lack of specialist education for children with autism in the UK. Based in London, the charity pilots, evaluates and disseminates nationally a range of services which support children affected by autism, their families and professionals working in the field of autism education.

Funding requirement

TreeHouse has an annual turnover of £4 million, of which 75 per cent is funded by fees from local education authorities and the remainder funded through an annual revenue fundraising campaign. In addition, TreeHouse has a major building appeal, Ambitious about Autism, with a target of £11.5 million and once that is concluded will have an ongoing need to support minor capital projects.

The case for support

There are a number of key factors that support TreeHouse's fundraising proposition:

> **The cause.** Autism is a complex communication disorder. Although there is limited understanding of autism, there is great intrigue about the condition.
>
> **The need.** Education is the only intervention which is proven to support the development of children with autism, yet there is a huge shortfall in the number of appropriate school places and teachers with adequate training.
>
> **The impact.** There is significant evidence proving that children with autism do not do well in life, which places a huge and unnecessary emotional burden on families and places a financial cost on the public purse.
>
> **The response.** TreeHouse's response, testing and then sharing new approaches to autism education, is clear and the charity can clearly evidence the positive impact on its beneficiaries.
>
> **The projects.** TreeHouse's services are all innovative and most are self financing once fully established. In addition, TreeHouse can offer funders a mix of: revenue and capital needs; local and national services; and short-, medium- and long-term projects.
>
> **The audience.** Due to the high prevalence (autism affects 1 child in every 100), most people will have a relative, or know a family, affected by autism.

These are all clearly articulated and evidenced in TreeHouse's 'case for support', a key tool that the charity uses across its fundraising, albeit adapted for different audiences.

Fundraising strategy

Growth and diversification

TreeHouse's fundraising requirement has increased along with the charity's rapid growth. Additionally, the sources of funds have increasingly diversified. In the early days, TreeHouse was heavily reliant on donations from a small number of major donors. Having systematically invested in developing, first, trust, lottery and statutory fundraising, followed by community, events, corporate and major donor fundraising, TreeHouse now has a broad portfolio of supporters within each of these income streams.

TreeHouse's fundraising strategy focuses on two priorities. First, to grow the total income from each income stream to meet TreeHouse's growing need for voluntary income and, second, to ensure that within each income stream we continue to recruit new, and develop the value of, donors.

Fundraising team

Each of the team of 12 fundraisers specialises in one of the following fundraising:

- trusts, lottery and statutory
- individuals (regular gifts) and community groups
- individual donors (major gifts)
- corporate
- events.

In addition, the fundraising team has a project coordinator, who is responsible for liaising with TreeHouse service delivery staff to ensure that their plans are packaged into projects for the fundraisers to pitch, and the finance department to ensure that restricted funds are monitored. The project coordinator also plays a key role in ensuring that projects are delivered according to the donors' restrictions and that the outcomes and impact of TreeHouse's projects are evaluated and articulated.

Although TreeHouse fundraisers each specialise, flexibility is retained regarding which fundraiser may work with a particular donor. For example, a corporate fundraiser may work directly with a major donor, if they are the chief executive of a company with which the fundraiser has developed a strong relationship. Similarly, if a trustee of a local trust is considering making a major legacy pledge, the trust fundraiser with whom they have worked will lead the administration.

The decision regarding who should lead the relationship is always led by the answer to the question 'Who has the strongest connection with the person making the decision to give a gift?' This sounds incredibly obvious but it is common to hear of fundraisers being led by the fundraising mechanic in which they are expert, rather than what the relationship with the donor requires.

Implications of being donor led

Of course there are a number of implications of this practice. The first is that while fundraisers may specialise, they need to have a good understanding of all fundraising disciplines. This is met through a range of internal and external training and frequent team brainstorming. In addition, great emphasis is placed on the fundraisers knowing about the autism cause and organisation, so that they can talk, with confidence, about TreeHouse to any type of audience.

The team also needs to have very good communication so that each fundraiser knows which prospects their colleagues are approaching. This is managed through recording details of planned approaches on TreeHouse's database and through a monthly verbal update from each fundraiser to the rest of the team. The fundraisers also frequently brainstorm specific donor strategies. For example, the corporate fundraiser may have excellent ideas about organising a lunch to warm trust contacts.

The fundraisers spend time preparing lists featuring corporate, trust or individual prospects, which are circulated among the fundraising team, senior staff and TreeHouse trustees. Each fundraiser will use the list when speaking with the donors with which they are working. For example, a corporate fundraiser recently took a prospect list to an update meeting with the chief executive of a corporate supporter, and he arranged to introduce her to the chairman of a major trust, with which we had no other relationship.

In terms of account management, there are often a number of fundraisers involved in supporting a relationship. The lead fundraiser is the person who has the strongest relationship with the funder, not who leads the fundraising mechanic. Where specific technical expertise is required, for example a trust fundraiser working with a potential legator, the trust fundraiser may front the relationship with strong technical direction from the individuals fundraiser. In time, it may be appropriate for the individuals fundraiser to be slowly and carefully introduced into the relationship but this must be informed by the lead fundraiser with the best understanding of the donor. Finally the lead fundraiser may also require some senior support, from a trustee or the chief executive. These individuals are often asked to host initial meetings or visits and be involved in the thanking process. However, usually the lead fundraiser will provide a briefing about exactly what is required from the senior colleague in such a scenario.

Finally, the structuring of TreeHouse's income targets reflects TreeHouse's way of integrated working. Although the charity establishes clear expectations for income from each donor group, the targets are not attached to individual fundraisers: the TreeHouse fundraising target is a team target. To support this, the team has a high degree of understanding of TreeHouse's overall financial strategy and clarity about TreeHouse's revenue and capital funding requirements. In addition there is understanding of the income expectations from each donor group and a shared understanding of the work required to support each income stream. The team has a weekly update on donations received and on a monthly basis review performance against income target. This clarity of TreeHouse's financial position and progress towards the fundraising target nurtures a collective responsibility for meeting the priorities of TreeHouse's fundraising strategy.

Integration of corporate fundraising

The fundraisers at TreeHouse manage relationships with any type of funder using the seven-step donor cultivation cycle, common in major gift fundraising. These are:

- identify
- research
- strategise
- cultivate
- ask
- acknowledge
- involve.

The following sections explain how, at each part of the cycle, there is focus on integration, to the benefit of all income streams.

Identifying possible supporters

When identifying a possible supporter, the fundraisers at TreeHouse are encouraged to think about the network in which the donor is placed. For example, a corporate prospect may be well networked and could be key to opening the door to a range of other prospects. The fundraisers are considered to think about supporting their own but also colleagues' income streams. The chart below demonstrates the network of A Company Ltd. The company is a corporate donor but could also influence gifts from other companies, individuals, high net worth individuals or trusts which would support a number of income streams. Each one of A Company's contacts also sits in the centre of its own network. At TreeHouse, the fundraisers prioritise researching and recording information about this network. This helps fundraisers to strategise their approach (see below, 'Strategising the approach') to both A Company and also to other prospects in A Company's network.

FIGURE 11.1 NETWORK SURROUNDING A DONOR COMPANY

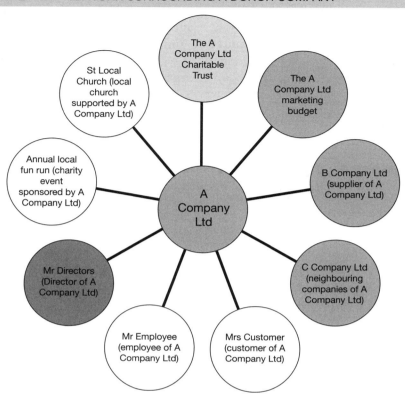

Researching prospects

It is important to complete rigorous and extensive prospect research on both the donor you are targeting and their networks. Desk research can reveal crucial information. For example, TreeHouse was once being considered as beneficiary of a major media appeal and through Internet research, a fundraiser established that one of TreeHouse's key corporate supporters was a major buyer of advertising in the newspaper. While a fundraiser should not expect TreeHouse's supporter to influence the outcome of the media appeal, they were able to ensure that the application was given full consideration: a major coup when TreeHouse's proposal was received alongside several hundred others.

Additionally at TreeHouse, the fundraisers make huge efforts to get out and speak to people. Through informal conversations with supporters and by showing interest in their world, it is possible to gather vital information to inform an approach. For example, during a chance conversation with a trustee of one of TreeHouse's trust funders, he mentioned that his employer was considering reviewing their giving guidelines and so TreeHouse was able to submit an application to the company, even before the new giving criteria were promoted. The TreeHouse fundraisers always assume that if a contact is supporting the cause, they want to help and they are therefore willing to provide information and open up their networks.

The TreeHouse fundraisers do not underestimate the value of talking to other fundraisers. They attend networking events, special interest groups and approach people at training events and conferences, all of which can be a fruitful source of leads and information. Be willing to share experiences about your successes and failures and you will generate information in return.

Finally, experience has shown that charities that have been previously supported by a donor that a fundraiser is researching, will often provide pertinent information. This is the case in particular where a company adopts a new charity each year. The previous beneficiary is often willing to talk about their experience of pitching and managing the partnership. In this way, fundraisers have often established information about what the funder is looking for which is not publicly available, giving TreeHouse's pitch a head start.

Strategising the approach

At this stage, you now know who your target is, what they do, what they are and are not interested in, who they know, who influences them and who they influence. Using this information, you can now start to plan how you will use your existing networks to develop a relationship.

At TreeHouse, the lead fundraiser will often complete and circulate the prospect research and invite colleagues to a brief meeting to brainstorm ideas on progressing the relationship. There are times when the fundraiser may also involve other donors in this, for example TreeHouse has supporters that work in marketing and they have given pro bono support to develop corporate fundraising pitches.

Usually the strategy will be multi-faceted. The fundraiser will always establish the formal process for approaching a possible donor, for example completing a corporate charity of the year application form. It is essential to comply with the formal application process.

It is also possible to have a parallel strategy which will involve developing a relationship with key influencers. Our fundraisers consider all the stakeholders they have identified as part of the prospect's network. Questions asked may include: Do we know any of the prospect's key advisors (lawyer, accountant, advertising agency or banker)? Do we know any of the prospect's key customers or suppliers? Are any directors of the company on our database, having made a donation or attended an event?

Cultivating the contact

The TreeHouse fundraiser will now start to implement what is likely to be a two-pronged strategy.

Following the donor's formal guidelines, the fundraiser will make a formal approach to the named correspondent: perhaps the company's Director of Corporate Social Responsibility, or a trust's Administrator. This approach could be made by the lead fundraiser, but on some occasions it may be appropriate to ask the Chief Executive, Chairman, a high-profile supporter, a volunteer or a beneficiary. The fundraiser will make this decision based on who might best influence the prospect.

At TreeHouse this initial approach will always include a request for a meeting to discuss the impending application and where possible to hold this initial meeting at the charity's site. The fundraiser will prepare thoroughly for such visits with a plan of how they intend to present the work, usually through a tour of the project followed by a meeting and introductions to key people. Alternatively, the fundraiser will meet the prospect at their office and work hard to engage the contact, infect them with enthusiasm for the cause and ensure that they remember TreeHouse when the final application is being considered.

This first meeting is an opportunity to gather as much information as possible about what the prospect is looking to see in an application and who is involved in the decision-making process. You are likely to establish valuable information to complement your existing prospect research.

The second element of the cultivation is to 'warm' the key influencers. At TreeHouse this 'warming' may involve an existing contact making a call or writing a letter to a high-level prospect. This approach works well where the ask made of the individual is small, for example 'Could you spare an hour to hear about TreeHouse, an amazing organisation that is very important to me?' or 'I would be grateful if you could see that TreeHouse's application is properly considered, I know that they would be an excellent recipient of your support.'

The cultivation process may take a long time and so it is crucial to maintain the relationships that have been developed. The fundraisers at TreeHouse use newsletters, always sent with a personalised covering letter, to update donors and influencers. They also invite contacts to events and share press cuttings featuring TreeHouse or the autism cause.

Asking for a gift

When the cultivation process has reached the appropriate stage, the donor will be ready to be asked for a donation. The fundraiser will know to ask for the right amount, for the right project, at the right time and most importantly, the ask will be made by the best possible person. If the fundraiser has been able to access them, the person or people who are the key influencers of the gift will know about the cause and should be inclined to consider the application favourably.

The way in which the ask is made will depend on the outcome of the prospect research and cultivation. It may be a letter, an application, a presentation pitch or a face-to-face meeting. Whatever form it takes, the fundraisers make sure that TreeHouse applications stand out from the others. The request may include photographs, case studies from families, supporter testimonies and sometimes even tailor-made story books.

The fundraiser will contact the correspondent to make sure that the submission has been received and promptly supply any further information required.

Acknowledging the support

Once the fundraiser has heard the outcome of an approach they will arrange appropriate acknowledgement.

Even if the ask has not generated a gift, it is incredibly important to appropriately thank the prospect for considering the approach and thank each of the contacts who used their networks to progress the approach. The fundraiser will contact TreeHouse's friends and keep them informed of the outcome. At TreeHouse the fundraisers have known contacts to get so excited about securing a gift from a member of their network that, if the charity receives a rejection, TreeHouse's contacts have proactively sought out alternative possible supporters.

If the ask has been rejected, the fundraiser will always try to secure a meeting to discuss the request and gather feedback on the strengths and weaknesses of the application. It is an excellent opportunity to improve future applications, discuss other opportunities for the prospect to support TreeHouse, ideally including introductions to their networks, and prepare the way for a future approach.

Involving the donor

If the outcome of the ask has secured a donation or a partnership, then TreeHouse has an opportunity to cement a long-term relationship. Even if the level of support is modest, the fundraiser assumes that there is always the possibility of further support. For example, TreeHouse was once supported by a company with a strict charity of the year policy. During the year the fundraisers cemented the relationship so well that they agreed to offer significant ongoing pro bono professional services.

At TreeHouse, the fundraisers will always feed back how any donation has been used and the impact that it has had on children with autism and their families. TreeHouse produces feedback reports, sends photo albums and invites donors to visit so that the fundraiser can demonstrate what the donor's funding has achieved. The fundraisers also offer feedback presentations, particularly where employees have been involved in the fundraising. On one occasion a fundraiser delivered a presentation to a small group of employees who had raised a modest sum for TreeHouse. It later transpired that the company's most senior member of staff had attended and he proceeded to build a relationship with the fundraiser and then introduced her to a trust which made a gift of half a million pounds.

Involving the donor will ensure that the donor feels part of the TreeHouse family and that they can play a significant role in changing the world for children with autism and they will continue to do so.

Summary

TreeHouse has worked hard to develop a fundraising culture that is led by the relationship that the donor requires and not the fundraising mechanic. The team has a huge knowledge of the charity and all fundraising disciplines, to ensure that they can engage any donor at any level, and maximise every opportunity that they come across. This approach has been essential in working with supporters to gain access to other supporters, feeding a number of income streams and meeting the team's fundraising target.

CHAPTER TWELVE

Ethical policies
A case study of Diabetes UK

Helen Hirons

Ethics of working relationships policy

Background to the policy

As the largest diabetes charity in the country, Diabetes UK decided several years ago to adopt an ethics policy to guide its working relationships with the corporate sector. Diabetes UK wanted to ensure that all partnerships were as open and transparent as possible and reflected the overall ethics and brand values of the charity. The policy formed the cornerstone of a strategy to invest greater resources in corporate fundraising and extend beyond established links with the pharmaceutical industry. Diabetes UK had traditionally gained sponsorship for specific areas of work and wanted to open up new revenue streams such as charity of the year partnerships and payroll giving.

Rationale of the policy

The need for a framework for working with companies became increasingly important as the complexity of corporate partnerships expanded and the level of income from individual companies increased. Diabetes UK wanted to recognise the importance of partnership working to the charity not only in terms of income but to raise awareness of diabetes and membership of Diabetes UK and to develop information and support that they would not be able to provide alone. It was also important to reduce the risks associated with corporate partnerships such as bad PR or an adverse reaction from individual supporters and members. A policy would allow corporate fundraisers to identify and assess risks within guided parameters.

Drafting a working policy

Critical questions were asked in order to develop a robust working policy that was accessible and covered a variety of situations. Stakeholders were consulted as part of the process to take their views into account when drafting the policy. This was also an opportunity to formalise the many excellent working practices already being undertaken by staff and act as a key guide in evaluating whether to work in partnership when proactively approaching companies.

Key issues to be considered were:

- Ensuring the policy fitted in with organisational values – Do the values and ethics of the company complement the charity? Is there a conflict of brand values? Does the company discriminate against people with diabetes?

- Confirming integrity, openness, independence, equality and responsibility – Is it a fair exchange and a mutually beneficial partnership? Are the benefits to Diabetes UK of an equal value to those received by the company?

- Consistency of the policy with other procedures and policies within the charity and externally such as the Charities Act or the ABPI (Association of the British Pharmaceutical Industry) guidelines. Fundraisers as well as companies need to be aware of the boundaries they operate within in order to avoid a conflict of interest or refusal of a donation at a later stage.

- Maintaining independence – ensuring that the reputation or credibility of Diabetes UK are not jeopardised and that the risks do not outweigh the potential benefits to people with diabetes. Larger donations from one company or from a range within one industry sector could lead to allegations of bias, so clear guidance of what would be an acceptable level is needed.

The policy in practice

The charity's Ethics of Working Relationships Policy was formally adopted by the board of trustees in 2002 and is available to download on the Diabetes UK website. An approval process is in place to ensure the policy is followed whenever a new corporate partnership is proposed. This takes the form of a risk assessment by key specified staff who analyse the nature of the partnership and test whether it meets the requirements of the policy. Where specialist help is required, for example in the case of a footwear company, a podiatrist is consulted, either internally or via an advisory committee. The process is clearly defined, with a form for staff to check and sign if they deem the relationship can be developed further.

Fundraisers are able to assess for themselves in advance whether the relationship is likely to fall within the policy and can make an informed decision when proactively approaching companies.

The main features of the policy are:

- Diabetes UK will not work with
  - companies that are directly connected with the tobacco industry
  - products not proven to be of benefit for people with diabetes, e.g. 'diabetic foods' such as confectionary
  - products deemed to be detrimental to people with diabetes, such as products claiming health benefits without scientific evidence.

- Only 5 per cent of total income per annum will be accepted from a partner with a vested interest in diabetes.

- Only 20 per cent of total income will be accepted from commercial organisations with a vested interest in diabetes.

- Employee fundraising such as charity of the year initiatives or payroll giving are excluded from the policy as the funds are raised by staff rather than corporate money.

- All partnerships worth £100,000 or above will need additional sign-off by the senior management team and the board of trustees.

- The main policy has a number of appendices which cover aspects of corporate fundraising in more details, such as advertising in Diabetes UK's publications.

The policy is very much a working document, used on a daily basis to guide the workings of the corporate fundraisers and others such as the health care and policy teams. It is reviewed and updated regularly to ensure it remains relevant to current working practices and meets the current needs of the charity. For example, the policy originally stated that all relationships worth more than £50,000 required senior management and board of trustees sign-off but, as corporate fundraising has grown within the charity, the level was raised.

Monitoring and compliance

At the end of every financial year a report is compiled by the Head of Corporate Fundraising for the board of trustees to illustrate how the charity has complied with the policy. This includes all income received from external organisations, including gifts in kind, as well as a breakdown of total income received from specific sectors such as the pharmaceutical sector.

Conclusion

Diabetes UK set out to develop a policy which would help both corporate supporters and staff within the charity to manage mutually beneficial relationships. The policy has now been in place for several years and is used daily to provide a framework within which such relationships continue to develop and grow. Ensuring the policy is adhered to by a rigorous risk assessment and reporting process allows the policy to be a living document which can be updated to reflect current working practices.

On-pack promotions policy

Background to the policy

Diabetes UK already had an Ethics of Working Relationships Policy in place when it expanded the policy to include on-pack promotions or cause-related marketing. The charity believed that this was an area it needed to explore to maximise income from the corporate sector, if the associated risks could be minimised. It would also be an opportunity to reach a wider audience of people with diabetes, increase membership and generally increase the profile of the charity.

Diabetes UK was careful to ensure its stakeholders were consulted and undertook a survey of its members. The results showed a largely pragmatic approach to the issue and recognition of the need to raise money and awareness of the cause. The charity decided to trial on-pack promotions on low-risk products not directly associated with the cause in order to develop and test a thorough risk assessment process for specific promotions

Rationale of the policy

Diabetes approved its Ethics of Working Relationships Policy in 2002 and by 2004 felt it was time to review elements of the policy in the light of the general increase in cause-related marketing, the increasing number of product promotion opportunities for Diabetes UK and a recent successful pilot on-pack promotion with Morrisons, as part of a charity of the year partnership.

Diabetes UK hoped that the policy would help increase the number and variety of fundraising opportunities available and widen the scope of its corporate fundraising. It aimed to:

• increase income, reach a wider audience, increase awareness of diabetes and Diabetes UK

• fund large-scale health awareness campaigns

- fund additional Diabetes UK services
- increase Diabetes UK membership through targeted promotions
- increase the database for future fundraising appeals.

Drafting a working policy

One of the main concerns of the charity was managing risks associated with on-pack promotions and the highly visible link of the charity to a product. Diabetes UK aimed to put a comprehensive process in place designed to minimise the risks of the activity, while maximising the income-generating opportunities that arose. Diabetes UK needed to identify possible risks associated with specific on-pack promotions, assess the level of risk and put in place actions to manage the risks, where appropriate.

Key issues considered were:

- Does the product meet industry standards or kite marks?

- Could a consumer misinterpret the presence of the Diabetes UK logo?

- Will Diabetes UK policy messages be undermined, such as healthy eating messages?

- Might members or donors object to the Diabetes UK logo being on the pack?

- Could there be a negative impact on the reputation of Diabetes UK, e.g. product recall?

- Have legal implications been identified, such as insurance and indemnities?

The policy in practice

A four-level approval process was introduced to identify whether a proposed on-pack promotion should be progressed and was in line with the policy.

Levels 1 and 2 involve appropriate heads of team across the organisation to ascertain level of risk, for example, to reputation, income potential and awareness opportunities.

Level 3 involves the Marketing Opportunity Group, which meets to measure the activity against the current policy and formally sign off the activity. To ensure transparency and objectivity, decisions are made using a decision tree which asks relevant questions pertinent to various sections of the policy. The group is made up of staff who have expertise in the various areas of the policy, such as health care, and is chaired by the Head of Corporate and Community Fundraising.

In exceptional circumstances (level 4), a decision may be referred to the board of trustees. If at any level, a decision cannot be made, the decision is referred to the next level.

The key features of the policy are:

- A robust risk assessment process to ensure promotions are approved and managed to the highest standards.

- The risk to reputation of working with a specific company will always be assessed.

- No on-pack partnerships can be entered into for tobacco or alcohol.

- No promotion if a food product contradicts a Diabetes UK health policy message.

- Fundraisers always ensure that the company provides evidence that a specific product adheres to industry or kite mark standards.

- Diabetes UK then uses the same process to access the risk of working with that product.

- Diabetes UK will supply clear wording of the working relationship and agree this with the company before proceeding.

- Contracts to ensure adherence to the policy and other legal considerations are issued once the level of risk is accessed and deemed acceptable.

Monitoring and compliance

Each approved activity is formally signed off by the Marketing Opportunity Group, using a specially designed form. At the end of the financial year a report is compiled by the Head of Corporate and Community Fundraising for the board of trustees to illustrate how the charity has complied with the Ethics Of Working Relationships Policy and the on-pack policy

Conclusion

On-pack promotions are one of the many ways Diabetes UK works with companies to raise funds, raise awareness of the cause and engage directly with the general public. The policy ensures that risks are assessed and evaluated within guidelines, before proceeding with a project. This gives both staff and companies a framework within which they can work and fulfil objectives.

CHAPTER THIRTEEN

The pitching process – BAE Systems

James Hayward

Pitching to be a company's partner charity can often be a daunting experience, especially as corporate charity schemes can differ greatly. Some like to focus completely on fundraising targets – it is something that every employee can relate to because it is embedded within their corporate culture. Some are only interested in the cause and are happy to organise virtually all their fundraising activities themselves. And others see it as an important human resources tool to help train staff while also helping charity at the same time.

BAE Systems' Charity Challenge

BAE Systems' Charity Challenge falls into the latter of these categories as the company primarily sees its charity partnerships as an employee development tool, with both fundraising and volunteering as being equally as important. In fact, when BAE Systems started its Charity Challenge scheme in 1989, it was seen as an under-25s development tool to help provide opportunities for young people to develop skills in communication, team working, networking, negotiation, leadership and project management. The scheme proved to be such a success that everyone in the company wanted to join in and it was launched as a global initiative.

BAE Systems' Charity Challenge has grown from strength to strength, developing staff, with one employee even receiving an MBE for their charity work, and raising millions of pounds backed up by thousands of volunteer days to help charities. For example, during the 2005/06 UK campaign, employees raised almost £3 million and volunteered 3,500 days for charity. These totals include 3,000 volunteered days and £1 million for the Stroke Association which was the partner charity for the 18-month campaign.

The process for selecting the BAE Systems' partner charity is entirely down to employees. It starts with a nomination route, whereby staff submit the names of any charities they would like to work with. This brings in a vast selection of names which have to be sorted through, to remove any that don't suit the criteria – they must have national representation, they must be able to offer volunteering opportunities, they must have locations near BAE Systems' sites and they must be big enough to handle the partnership.

The next step is to send application forms to each charity, posing questions and asking for examples of how the charity would meet the challenge of being BAE Systems' partner charity. The replies are then sent to a judging panel made up of employees, who select approximately ten charities to pitch to the panel. Via the pitching process, the number of charities is narrowed down to five. Employees are then invited to cast their vote to choose which of the five they would like to work with for the next 18-month campaign.

In the BAE Systems selection process, the most significant time for the charities to influence the vote is during the pitching stage. However, it could be argued that filling in the written application is just as important, although in the case of BAE Systems, it is more about giving information about the charity and how it works, while the pitch brings the application to life and bridges the gap between the charity and the company to demonstrate how they can work together.

Preparing for the pitch

Research

A key thing to remember when you start putting together your pitch is that every company's charity structure has the potential to be very different from the next. A good understanding of what the company needs and wants is crucial, before you decide what you can offer. Think of the pitch as a product, which needs careful market research to make sure it meets the individual needs of the customer. Too often, the judging panel for BAE Systems' hears a pitch that that comes across as a group of people going through the motions, with little demonstrable attempt to personalise the presentation and possibilities that are available with the partnership.

One way to carry out your research is to talk to the people who are involved with charity work for the company. This can be either someone working centrally on the partnership who can spare the time or perhaps someone that one of your local groups may know at the company because they have raised money for them. They will appreciate being asked to give their input, especially if their advice makes for a better partnership were you to be selected. Also, contact other charities that have worked with that company, as you will be able to learn from their experiences. Either way, it is often easy to see which charities have talked to an employee or done some research, as they will clearly stand out.

Charity toolkit

As mentioned above, the pitch is your opportunity to bring to life your written application and to link what the charity can offer, the research on what the company wants and how you can bring it all together to create a great partnership. During pitches to BAE Systems, the panel is always keen to hear about what the charity can offer across the board. This doesn't just include fundraising and volunteering, but also services such as publicity, payroll-giving promotion and production of bespoke publicity material. For example, at a recent pitch, one charity discussed how it had created a department entirely designed to come up with new fundraising ideas and how to make them work to their maximum potential. This really impressed the BAE Systems panel, because often there is an element of risk with running any event and if that can be reduced in any way then it is a big help.

Presentation guideline

In preparing for your presentation, it is worth checking if the judging panel has any guidance they can give you regarding the pitch. BAE Systems, for example, always asks that charities leave out any emotional content from their pitch. This may sound callous, as this can be the most powerful part of any presentation, but it also has the ability to clear rooms. Before BAE Systems introduced this rule, panel members often had to leave the room during pitches because they were so moved. It can be very emotionally draining on the judges if this happens and their judgement can be clouded. The judges know the causes championed by charities, often personally, and rather than making emotional judgements, they become more objective and look upon the process as business pitch, where they are looking for the charity which fits the best.

At BAE Systems, once the judges have found five charities that meet the needs for their partnership, the employees get to vote. This is where the emotion comes in, as they can vote with their hearts, trusting the panel to have made the judgement required on matching up the right potential partnerships.

Choosing a presentation team

When you are considering who to invite along to the presentation, try to bring along a broad spectrum of people from different areas of your work. Many charities pitching to BAE Systems realise the importance of volunteering, so they bring along someone from that field, others have included an account manager who has experience working with other corporate charity partnerships with similar needs. Some charities bring along senior members. The panel will appreciate their presence, but on more than one occasion the executive has looked impatient and kept an eye on their watch. Once the presentation team has left the room, it is not just the pitch that is discussed – something like negative body language can be picked up easily and reflects badly on the overall presentation.

One of the best presentations for the BAE Systems' partnership, in terms of the team involved, was when one team member acted as the chair for a team of four people and controlled the flow of the presentation perfectly. This kept the presentation slick and smooth, with other team members being introduced at the appropriate moments. It also gave the panel a focal point for questions, which were then directed to the relevant team member. It left the panel with a very positive impression.

Another good example stands out – a pitch from an English and Scottish partnership charity, where the team acted like a double act. In the past, BAE Systems has been a little weary of these types of partnerships, due to the problems that have arisen with poor communication and little or no synergy between the two charities. In this example, it was as if the two charities understood these concerns and they demonstrated how they work closely together across both regions by sharing ideas and materials, goals and methods to achieve them. Their professional manner really helped to alleviate the panel's initial fears.

The pitch

Fundraising

When it comes to the presentation, the panel will be keen to see how you can best apply the various aspects of your charity to give the company the services it feels it needs. Again, this will depend dramatically on the company. BAE Systems is very eager for support from both the charity head office and the charity's regional offices, preferably based near its sites around the UK. The central support can drive countrywide activities while enabling the BAE Systems' Charity Challenge head office team to work with the charity directly. Meanwhile the regional offices will help the process of building up a relationship which will increase the emotive connection, give them direct contact with where the money is going and also opportunities for local volunteering projects.

It is also important to demonstrate what sorts of activities you have planned for volunteers. Anything that the charity is already doing is good to tap into, as there will be existing publicity, but the company will also want to hear about bespoke ideas. At BAE Systems, the judging panel likes to hear a range of ideas that vary in size as well as creativity. Tapping into already existing events is also popular. For example, if you are a cancer charity, it is worth linking in to Breast Cancer Awareness month and Bowel

Cancer Awareness week. If you can link them into big company events, then that is also encouraged. For example, BAE Systems has a large presence at the Farnborough International Airshow, which is held every two years. A charity could mention that a sponsored plane pull would be good to link into the event, as not only does it link into the company, it also gives the opportunity to have BAE Systems sites or businesses competing against each other – a good, and exciting, way to generate more money.

Volunteering

If the company is interested in getting involved with volunteering, it is good to talk to it about how important volunteers are to your organisation. Give it an idea of what sorts of opportunities already exist within the charity, while also talking about other ideas you think the company may be interested in. Try to give a broad spectrum of activities, from those requiring a low commitment level, like writing a letter to their local MP, all the way through to training as a counsellor on a helpline. At BAE Systems, gardening and decorating projects are extremely popular. They are easy to arrange and they are the sorts of activities that everyone, no matter their ability, can join in with. Every team needs someone who can make the tea or wash the brushes.

It is also important to discuss the advantages of volunteering as a way of developing staff. Many companies spend a large amount of money organising activities, such as paintballing, to help boost staff morale. Instead, they could save money and help charity by getting the staff into teams that compete against each other to decorate parts of a house in a *Changing Rooms* style, where the winner is the team that has done the best job. BAE Systems Charity Challenge's main goal is to develop staff: throughout the years, the benefits have been seen on many different levels. For example, helping out at a call centre or organising a decorating project can bring benefits to an employee's everyday role in such areas as communication, project management and team building.

Examples of previous or current corporate partners

It is always good to talk to the panel about your previous or current corporate partners and how these campaigns went. If your charity has a wide selection to choose from, try to mention a couple of impressive names, but also include an example of a company similar to the one you are pitching to. For example, it sounds great talking about working previously with Barclay's Bank or Sky but if there's a small company that you worked with that had similar needs to the company you are currently pitching to, include it as well. It is also good to offer references for your examples, as very often companies talk to each other about fundraising. For example BAE Systems' Charity Challenge team are part of a group made up of companies like Barclay's Bank, Argos, HBOS and Royal Mail among others, that try to get together once a quarter to talk and share experiences.

Feel-good factor

Creating a feel-good factor for the panel is a great way of showing that you are fun to work with and that the money that is raised will be put to good use. One presentation that was given to the BAE Systems panel recently really played on the fact that everyone at the charity was behind the pitch. They showed short videos of the members of the team at their head office saying how excited they were about the pitch and how much they were looking forward to working with the company. They also had a photo of the team outside the office waving the pitching team off and holding a big banner saying good luck. It left the panel with a good feeling – it was nice to know that everyone at the charity was supporting the four people in the room doing the pitch.

Finally...

Finally, all that is left is to answer a few questions and ask some of your own if you have any. Some good ones include: Would there be other ways of working with the company if you don't win the partnership? Is there any possibility of getting feedback on your pitch once the company has chosen its new partner? It is worth remembering that partnership opportunities will come around again and if you have impressed this time, you may be invited back again. And the next time you can be better prepared.

Key points

● **Know your audience** – All companies behave differently with their charitable activities, so it's important to do your research.

● **Have a diverse charity toolkit** – Look at all areas of your charity and think how a corporate partner might like to benefit from your services. This can be anything from your PR team, events team or design team to your previous corporate partner experience.

● **Know the presentation guidelines** – Be careful with emotional content, as you don't want to run the risk of emptying a room. Leaving thought-provoking items with the panel can be a great way of showing initiative and provide something for them to take away and think about.

- **Chose a good team to present** – They will be the face of the charity so choose calm, friendly people who know what they are talking about and can communicate ideas clearly and precisely.

- **Impress with your fundraising ideas** – Give examples of some ideas both big and small and also traditional and imaginative. Link them into already established events.

- **Demonstrate the importance of volunteering** – not just to the charity but how important it could be to the company.

- **Think carefully about discussing previous/current partners** – Big names sound impressive but it always good to mention someone who you feel has a similar charity set-up to the company you are pitching to.

- **Leave the panel feeling good** – Let them know that the charity is behind the pitch and how much difference winning this partnership could mean to your cause.

CHAPTER FOURTEEN

Marks & Spencer and Breakthrough Breast Cancer: no brief encounter

A case study in real partnership

Laurie Boult and Rachael Reeve

Breakthrough Breast Cancer (Breakthrough) and Marks & Spencer (M&S) have been partners since 2001 and to date have raised over £6.5 million through a creative mix of product marketing campaigns, employee fundraising and pink ribbons. The partnership holds the award for National Example of Excellence in Cause Related Business by Business in the Community.[10] This recognised the depth and breadth of the partnership which had grown from a tactical pin placement opportunity worth an annual £145,000 in 2001 to a primary cross-business marketing campaign, embedded in M&S's retail strategy for CSR and worth £1.4 million by 2005. It also recognised the ambition with which M&S and Breakthrough collaborated to develop the high street's first post-surgery lingerie offering from a major retailer – a campaign which was recently showcased at the Treasury's annual CSR summit as a best practice example of 'power in partnership'. This chapter will give focus to the post-surgery range, but first, looks at what makes the partnership so successful.

The following section headings were not necessarily earmarked as cornerstones of partnership strategy from day one and are not in any particular order. Looking back over recent years, though, these are the key themes that have underpinned every partnership activity and made it the success it is today.

---

10 Awarded in 2006. See www.bitc.org.uk

Breast cancer is currently the most common female cancer in the UK. Nearly 44,000 women are diagnosed with breast cancer each year in the UK and nearly 1 in 3 of all cases of cancers in UK women are breast cancer. (Source: CRUK, 2006)

Stating the obvious: Fit

It might be the most repeated tenet of corporate fundraising literature that having a good fit between corporate and charity is key for a partnership to be successful. Suffice to say the greatest area of fit between the organisations is customer profile. Over 80 per cent of breast cancers occur in women over 50 and Breakthrough's key target audience is women aged 40 and over, in order that we reach them in time with life-saving breast awareness messages. Correspondingly, the M&S core customer is a woman aged 45–65.

Core partnership value 1: Trust

In order for a company to make and sustain significant investment of staff time and organisational budget in a partnership with a charity, a complete level of trust must be established and maintained between both parties. Account management systems and processes were put in place from day one to ensure that Breakthrough always delivered against objectives, and where those objectives weren't met the reasons were clearly identifiable and generally acknowledged in advance as outside of direct control. Trust has played a key role throughout but was fundamental to the post-surgery range.

Core partnership value 2: Knowledge

It is easy for either a charity or a company to become frustrated with its partner if neither truly understands how the other operates. Understanding decision-making structures, business strategy, where one party fits within the others' organisational priorities and how partnership goals feed in to each parties' own business goals are essential if you want a fulfilling partnership.

Reading the press may not forewarn you of important news but it is essential if you want to keep your finger on the pulse of the business.

Modus operandi (1): Integrate and adapt

Strategically, make your cause as relevant to the business in as many ways as you can and build links and relationships in every area. Descending from strategy engage employees, suppliers, customers, advertising agencies and other relevant third parties. Networking through your key corporate contact to understand organisational structure and levels of buy-in is a must. In 2001, Breakthrough had one contact at M&S in a marketing department; by 2005, that had grown to over 100 head-office employees across marketing, design, buying, retail, e-commerce, and suppliers.

Bring extra value to your partner by taking the partnership directly to their colleagues once your contact has alerted them to the potential benefits of it. Pitching a cause-related marketing campaign with M&S may involve giving what is broadly the same presentation to a number of different marketing and product teams. This shouldn't seem like something out of the ordinary. Think about it, how difficult do you find it to get your own colleagues together for an internal meeting?

Modus operandi (2): Ambition and innovation

Companies do not stand still. If your partnership does not evolve and innovate solutions for that business, then it may become seen as outdated and irrelevant. Solutions could relate to areas of the business, such as advertising, customer service, employee relations, sales and supply chain. With each year of partnership we have added a new product to our activity, moving from pin campaigns to employee fundraising to on-pack promotion to central marketing campaigns, while moving out from a partnership initiated in the lingerie department to one that incorporates womenswear, food and home departments. A company will compete against its competition so – if you want the company to take you seriously – you should be competing against them too, and this will usually mean choosing to work exclusively with your partner, provided you feel you receive enough value in return.

Putting it into practice – delivering the post-surgery range

Despite our innovation in adapting the partnership year on year, it was women, ironically women affected by breast cancer, who felt excluded. Following our high-profile partnership campaigns of 2005, letters to both partners ensued: a call to action for a range of lingerie to meet the needs of women following breast surgery. Some context is needed here. At this stage, the major retailers on the high street offered limited options for post-surgery and no definitive range. Bras were predominantly white, unfeminine, heavily strapped and without matching items. Design was led by technical need over and above fashion trend, meaning choice and femininity were removed from the shopping experience. For most women, this was a devastating discovery at a physically and emotionally debilitating time.

Breakthrough had to resolve the alienation of women who had undergone breast surgery from its product marketing campaigns. As the M&S/Breakthrough partnership gained status, it was clear that we had an opportunity to address the issue. M&S had already made a bold move in incorporating the iconic pink ribbon into a version of the corporate logo used during the promotional period (replacing the ampersand) and with co-branded carrier bags peppering the high street the message was clear – breast cancer is an important issue to M&S. Breaking news about Kylie Minogue also gave the issue high media profile. While the timing felt right, both partners recognised the potential for spin around a retailer paying lip service to a topical issue. Needless to say the fit and mutual need was obvious.

In partnership, Breakthrough and M&S collaborated to produce a detailed questionnaire (around 40 questions) designed to garner feedback on all existing high street lingerie and, more pressingly, to clarify specific technical requirements for the product and fitting service. From 200 supporters' responses, Breakthrough collated a detailed report of recommendations. The results are too vast and diverse to summarise here, but they underpinned the emotional as much as the practical need and directed us even more firmly towards a collaborative approach.

What followed was fairly ground-breaking in terms of how corporate partners and charities usually integrate. A series of hands-on focus groups with all three stakeholders allowed 20 supporters to give honest, critical feedback on all existing product and to set out specifically how they expected M&S to deliver the range and train its fitters. It was a brave move for both partners, not least in terms of reputational risk. Breakthrough had to trust M&S to remain committed, open and sensitive to its supporters. Conversely, as an M&S partner, the charity faced a major challenge in managing its supporter's expectations around what could realistically be delivered.

Trust was key on all levels. Involving the end-user at every stage of the process was a defining success factor. The supporters (all, incidentally, M&S customers) had directional input on various aspects from product trials, through to the percentage donation to Breakthrough. A donation per product sold was always in our partnership plan, but we had to sense check it with the end-users to ensure it remained appropriate. Through this process, we had satisfied the needs of a representative group of customers and earned their trust, but we had no idea how this would transfer to the wider public. Even within this small group of representative women opinion varied and only through the unique discussion forums had we all found common ground. The major challenge, however, proved not to be in getting the product right, but in finding a woman to model it.

Supporters made a unanimous request for a model who had undergone breast surgery. A woman who had not would, in their mind, undermine the unique purpose of the range and alienate the very women who had informed it. Despite an intensive search (from both partners), finding such a model in time for the product launch proved impossible. The women were naturally disappointed, but our relationship management process guaranteed that we had their sympathy. Any disappointment was shared rather than directed at one party. Had M&S worked alone, that supporter sympathy could well have been cynicism.

It became increasingly clear that launching the range would require careful communication, particularly as M&S took a decision to make the product available in 10 key stores and to online customers. Supporters were naturally expecting to see it in all stores and initially saw this as a lack of commitment from M&S. It is worth pointing out that official statistics on the number of women who have had breast surgery in the UK did not exist, making it virtually impossible for M&S to forecast sales potential or for Breakthrough to make recommendations. That aside, M&S business practice is to launch *any* new product in ten key stores to manage product risk in a controlled way. However, both partners were acutely aware that this might not be enough to convince the general public, particularly in the context of a national PR campaign. The range was genuinely presented as a work in progress and a multitude of feedback options were offered, including a customer service email address, phone number, postal address and a personal contact at Breakthrough. Stores were geographically placed to provided the widest accessibility for the target market as well as online availability, ensuring the collection was available to those who preferred to purchase more discreetly. This was married with a tailored fitting service driven by feedback from the focus groups – 'empathy not sympathy please!' This approach allowed the partners to gather customer feedback in a very focused way, which could then be used to finesse the future range.

How and why it was successful

As partners, M&S and Breakthrough delivered the first unique post-surgery lingerie range available from a major high street retailer – a collection of twelve matching lingerie sets incorporating specialist features for women who had undergone breast surgery while remaining feminine and fashionable. The media response was phenomenal with national coverage in the *Sun, The Times, Mail on Sunday, Daily Telegraph* and a number of regional dailies, generating a flurry of positive calls to both partners, strong sales to follow and new fundraising revenue for Breakthrough. Through supporter engagement, we minimised the risk of disappointment, cynicism and product failure. This was only made possible given the level to which the relationship between Breakthrough and M&S had matured and the grounding we had put in to our Breast Cancer Awareness Month marketing campaigns. Where fit, trust, knowledge, integration, ambition and innovation are key – timing is too.

The result, many supporters have told us, has ultimately been life-changing.

'This is about being feminine, but it's also about being normal. The best thing about this new range is that I can go to M&S with my daughter, and both of us will come home with a set of lingerie.'[11]

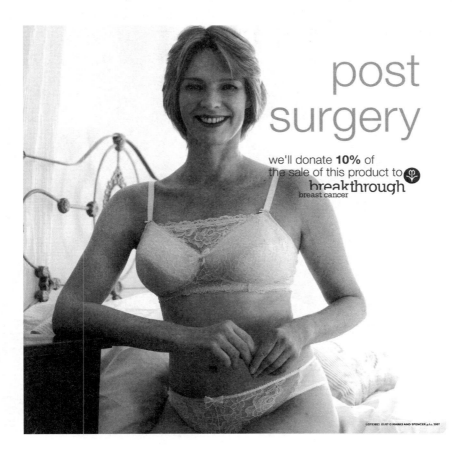

What future for the post-surgery range?

The range will continue to evolve and improve. The next collection (going to 16 stores) will expand to DD–G sizes with improvements on inner pocketing (to hold a prosthesis) and new on-trend colours, following further work and wearer trials with younger women. Swimwear has already been added and for the first time ever, post-surgery lingerie and swimwear will be included in the Fashion Targets Breast Cancer ® UK[12] campaign to

11 Pauline Ablitt, Breakthrough supporter and Post Surgery Feedback Group member.
12 Fashion Targets Breast Cancer® UK is Breakthrough's flagship fashion industry campaign, which raises money through the sale of distinctive target T-shirts. Marks &

provide a complete wardrobe of goods for women who have had breast cancer and breast surgery. At the time of writing, we have successfully engaged a professional lingerie model who fits in the 45+ category and has herself undergone reconstructive surgery following breast cancer: a significant step for both M&S and Breakthrough in delivering a product and service in a way that women expect it.

Spencer is one of a number of retailers producing licensed products for the campaign to raise money for Breakthrough. Fashion Targets Breast Cancer© is licensed by the Council of Fashion Designers of America / CFDA Foundation, Inc., USA.

CHAPTER FIFTEEN

Managing a charity of the year campaign – a case study of HBOS

Joan Hemmery

HBOS was formed from the merger of Halifax and Bank of Scotland in 2001 and employs around 70,000 people. Community investment forms a key part of the company's corporate responsibility strategy. Central to this is the HBOS Foundation set up in 2002 to provide a focus for community and charitable activity across the group.

Employee involvement underpins the role of the foundation. From an employee perspective, the main elements are:

- volunteering

- matched funds – where employees raise funds for their own charity and then get a proportion matched by HBOS

- Million £ Challenge – where employees raise at least £1m for the HBOS 'charity of the year'.

In the Million £ Challenge, the HBOS Foundation issues a challenge each year to all employees across the HBOS group to select a charity of the year from a shortlist of three and to raise at least £500,000 for the chosen charity. For each pound raised the HBOS Foundation matches the money – the Million £ Challenge. Any fundraising over the first £1 million is shared equally between all three short-listed charities.

The philosophy behind the creation of the Million £ Challenge was threefold:

- to create effective partnerships with community organisations which are not only sustainable but of mutual value

- to enthuse employees across the HBOS group about our community investment programme by focusing on a charity of interest to them

- to highlight the activity and work of the HBOS Foundation both internally and externally.

The Challenge provides an opportunity to engage directly with key stakeholders of the HBOS group which includes several large companies that are household names – Halifax, Bank of Scotland, Clerical Medical, Esure, Insight Investment and Intelligent Finance. The principal driver of the whole project – in addition to raising money for charity – is staff advocacy. The Million £ Challenge is an excellent tool to achieve that, through building staff pride in the organisation and commitment to it. The Challenge provides an opportunity for cross-group communication, collaboration and mutuality of interest that has helped build bridges between the various brands in a relatively new and young organisation. It is therefore a unique project embracing the whole organisation, creating common cause and boosting internal pride and brand advocacy. It is the only project which involves every single employee of the group.

Choosing the charities

Charities can apply direct; employees can nominate a charity; and charities are selected by the Foundation team, but the only charities considered are those that clearly demonstrate evidence of meeting all the following criteria.

- They must be a UK-wide registered charity, offering locally based services to the most vulnerable members of society.

- They must have experience of working in corporate partnerships and have the ability to construct, lead and manage a fundraising programme.

- They need to involve colleagues from HBOS group, including those recently retired, in fundraising activity the length and breadth of the country.

- They must have the capability of using the funds raised effectively across the UK, but with an emphasis on the 'local level' in towns where HBOS has a significant presence such as Edinburgh, Halifax or Bristol.

A significant feature of the project is the method of selection of the charity of the year. With nearly 21,000 colleagues participating in either intranet or telephone voting, the chosen charity is selected by staff and not, as is usually the case, by senior management or a committee. The charities feature in an internal business TV broadcast so that all HBOS staff can participate in the selection process. In 2005, the three short-listed charities were NSPCC/Children 1ST, Samaritans and Help the Aged.

Leadership and management

The HBOS Foundation is one of the truly group-wide activities in the organisation. It is backed by senior management, who are seen 'to walk the talk'. The chairman of the company has been featured on internal television taking part in an event, and other managers have been shown taking part in fundraising or volunteering activities.

The approach is through a carefully planned multi-media campaign.

The high-profile communication kicks off with the Million £ Challenge TV programme in January, where employees find out about the short-listed charities and then vote for the charity of the year. In 2005 this was presented by BBC's Natasha Kaplinsky. The HBOS business television network, one of the largest in Europe, is broadcast in all main employment centres and in 1,400 branches.

Anticipation of this has grown year on year and in January 2006 a record 25,500 colleagues voted. In its first year, 2003, the numbers voting were 15,000. The programme is broadcast at set times throughout the day via HBOS's business television network. In branches, it can be viewed during a training session; for central areas televisions are located on each floor. Employees then vote by the intranet or telephone.

Each division now actively promotes Foundation activity. Corporate division recently produced a CSR booklet for its employees and a specially commissioned video for its conference.

The Foundation team works closely with Group Internal Communications and divisional communicators in devising fundraising and communications plans which are updated quarterly and presented to the HBOS Foundation trustees. Board papers on the work of the Foundation and progress of the Challenge are presented to the HBOS group board and to divisional boards across the organisation throughout the year.

Management processes

From the outset each charity provides a simple direct Challenge which is communicated to employees; in 2005, this took the form:

• Help the Aged – to purchase special vehicles such as electric scooters and accessible minibuses

• NSPCC/Children 1ST – to provide dedicated therapeutic services to 750 children throughout the UK and help them recover from abuse

• Samaritans – to invest in new technology to ensure everyone seeking advice can always get through to a Samaritans counsellor.

HBOS is a very target-driven organisation and articulating a target for the Challenge in this way engages staff attention much more directly than the usual mode of communication on community projects. In an organisation which would usually regard community relations as important, but not the first priority, expressing the Challenge as a financial target is both arresting and effective. In a similar vein, the partner charities are asked to provide straightforward targets to describe how the money raised will be used by them. In relation to the simple targets set and the organisational objectives of improving staff morale, building cross-divisional relationships and developing colleague advocacy, the project has proved to be hugely successful.

Another key feature of the project is that all three charities benefit from the fundraising. This maintains as broad an interest in the project as possible, and maximises engagement and commitment to fundraising.

A team of 17 regional coordinators is fully involved in promoting and administering the Challenge and over 100 'Challenge champions' are identified across the group to provide a distribution and communications channel and to ensure that all colleagues who want to contribute and get involved are able to do so.

A fundraising plan, calendar of events and communications plan are developed in advance of the voting taking place each year. Each year a logo is designed and used on all the promotional posters and display materials.

The Challenge receives widespread communication coverage at group, divisional and local level. This is achieved through a multi-media approach. The company intranet carries news and support material and advertises activities such as raffles and fundraising events. The Challenge has its own bespoke intranet featuring information about how to get involved, fundraising events and the up-to-date fundraising figure. The internal magazine regularly carries Challenge news and Challenge Specials are issued at regular intervals to publicise specific events or to advise staff of exciting news or milestones reached.

Each fundraising activity – and this could be anything from a dress down day to a raffle for the Challenge – is given a detailed timeline and communication plan. One of the most popular events is a raffle to win an additional five days off work. Promotion of this usually entails all the media at our disposal from intranets to global emails.

The project is a continual learning process for those involved in managing it, many of whom knew little about fundraising when the project first began. At the end of the first year of the Million £ Challenge, a procedures manual was produced for future reference so that organisational learning was captured and maintained.

Many lessons were learned, for example:

- The need for greater preparation in advance of the launch of the charity of the year, so that fundraising commences immediately and no momentum is lost between the selection process and the first events.

- Create the short-list in the autumn and hold a series of meetings with the three charities so that they all know how the selection and management processes operate.

- Have the calendar of events ready for distribution as soon as the charity of the year is chosen.

Resources – from HBOS and charity partners

The Foundation team that manages and administers the project comprises five people who contribute a substantial part of their working time to the Million £ Challenge project.

The team is supported by the 'Challenge champions' and their regional coordinators. Challenge champions sell raffle tickets, collect at various events, orchestrate their own fundraising events and participate in the various activities which take place throughout the year.

Raffle prizes and objects/experiences for online auctions are provided at nil cost by managers and colleagues of the organisation, internal procurement and supply chain partners. The additional budget is provided by HBOS to meet the cost of fundraising events, activities and projects.

The charity of the year provides additional support to the Foundation team. The Challenge team is set up at the beginning of each year and regular fortnightly meetings take place which include charity of the year representatives and other colleagues from across the group, as required. NSPCC/Children 1ST required four members of their staff to support and motivate HBOS employees across the UK. However, in this respect charity expenditure is minimised because of the use of Challenge champions.

The charity provides promotional items, such as balloons and T-shirts, to HBOS locations when local fundraising activity takes place. Pin badges for the charities are offered for sale in the branch network.

Charity representatives visit offices on the last Friday of each month to collect funds, give advice on fundraising and stimulate interest and involvement.

Communication and dialogue

Communication is a fundamental feature of the project. Primarily aimed at HBOS employees, the project also involves customers and shareholders, a feature which will develop more in future years. Videos, television,

127

intranet, group-wide emails and divisional publications are all used to promote and provide news about the Challenge. Research from previous communication activity tells us that employees prefer a multi-media approach. For example, in a branch environment, the information-on-demand intranet may be more convenient than television broadcasts at set times.

On this basis, global emails are used for short messages to raise awareness of a subject and this is backed up with a link to more in-depth information on websites or in *HBOS Today*, the electronic group-wide magazine. Divisionally, local angles are provided for stories.

Management conferences and team away days are useful forums for communicating news about the Challenge and for fundraising activities. Where possible a video is shown at those events. Managers with high staff complements are encouraged to use the opportunities presented by the Challenge for morale building and motivation, as well as fundraising.

Customers are advised about the Challenge and invited to make contributions at various events, such as paying a small amount for a cup of coffee (normally provided free) in branches.

HBOS shareholders are invited to make contributions. For example, shareholders were offered the opportunity to contribute to the Challenge any small balances of under £2 left over from SCRIP offers.

A charity Christmas card is designed and produced each year to raise money for the Challenge. This is the company's corporate card, which means all business areas contribute to fundraising. It is also sold to staff across the Group and is a key Challenge fundraising activity each year.

Local MPs, MSPs and members of the Welsh Assembly are notified whenever key events are taking place in their constituencies. For example, the Christmas card each year is designed by the child of an HBOS employee. On one occasion, the MP for the constituency where the child lived participated in a photocall for local newspapers. Press releases on newsworthy achievements of the Challenge are released regularly.

At the end of the calendar year, an awards ceremony hosted by HBOS rewards those employees who have made an outstanding community contribution. The event celebrates the achievements of the Challenge in promoting fundraising and volunteering and provides a forum for the handover of the £1 million to NSPCC/Children 1ST.

In summary, the communication objectives are to:

- create a sense of excitement about community initiatives

- get employees involved

- help the charities through fundraising or volunteering

- improve employee advocacy about the way they view the organisation

- provide a high profile for the various initiatives.

Challenges faced

The original challenge was to convince employees and the business of the merits of the community programme. They have now seen the benefits.

Now the key issue is keeping things fresh, so that means coming up with new promotions/competitions to get employees involved.

It is important to gauge the right amount of communication and that this does not overshadow business communication or allow charity fatigue to set in.

Year on year the bar rises on fundraising targets for the Million £ Challenge.

Measurement of success

Community activity is now part of the culture of the organisation and society benefits from this investment in the community.

Working through a mix of centrally organised projects and local fundraising, in 2005 the £1 million target was achieved in six months. Thereafter money raised was split between the three short-listed charities. The sum finally raised at the end of the year amounted to £2.3m million (after matching). Of this,

- £1.2m went to NSPCC/Children 1ST, to provide therapeutic services at 43 projects around the UK for abused children

- over £230,000 each went to Samaritans and Help the Aged

- £750,000 went to the tsunami appeal.

Employee attitudes to community activity and CR are measured by MORI at least two times a year. In the 2005 opinion survey, 79 per cent of colleagues said they would speak highly about HBOS's charity and community activity and 67 per cent were positive about volunteering – up from 50 per cent.

After the Million £ Challenge television show, 85 per cent of colleagues said they thought the Challenge was a good thing and 61 per cent said it made them feel more positively about HBOS.

The end result is a sustained strategic campaign with measurable business and social impact, and a well-regarded initiative, which has provided the organisation with focus and 'corporate glue'.

Impact

The HBOS Foundation has provided a focus for the organisation's charitable and community activities and helps to improve colleague and employer advocacy. The Million £ Challenge is firmly embedded in HBOS culture.

Business benefits

A key focus of the HBOS Foundation is to help integrate the businesses within local communities. Internally, it has united colleagues behind a common goal especially when it comes to fundraising for the charity of the year.

The main benefits to the business were the improvement in the motivation and loyalty of colleagues, in particular,

- increased awareness and understanding of community investment
- improved colleague advocacy
- increased numbers participating in events
- increased fundraising
- increased volunteers
- heightened profile of the Foundation.

Staff attitude surveys have monitored the appreciation of employees of the Challenge and this has shown an improvement over the year. In the annual MORI opinion survey, 79 per cent of colleagues said they would speak highly of HBOS's charity and community activity. This question was asked again in October to a sample of colleagues and the positive response rose to 81 per cent.

The annual survey also saw increases in employer advocacy and pride in working for HBOS – areas influenced by community activity.

After the 2006 Million £ Challenge television show, 88 per cent of colleagues said they thought the Challenge was a good thing and 64 per cent said it made them feel more positively about HBOS.

Organised events, such as group-wide quizzes in Halifax, Edinburgh and Bristol bring hundreds of staff from different parts of the company together who would not otherwise have the opportunity to meet. The culmination of this in 2005 was a Guinness world record being set in Leeds for mass participation.

Employees across HBOS have learned a great deal about the art of fundraising. They have been encouraged to undertake volunteering and to get involved in projects which have improved their level of fitness (such as participating in fun runs and sponsored walks) and they have also improved their skills in getting involved community projects.

• The coordinators benefit from developmental opportunities and their activities are recognised in annual appraisals. Many have reported an increase in confidence and profile.

• The project has made an important contribution to our CR activities and to the level of our community investment.

• We are able to align the Challenge with our marketing activity to raise money from customers, which raises awareness of our charitable activity and the money raised for charity.

• The Challenge works alongside our sports sponsorships as we raise money at football and rugby matches where one of the group companies is main sponsor.

On a more general level, we are seeing more employees actively engaged in community activity. There has been a trend towards swapping traditional away days for more community-focused events.

We are advised by staff that contributions made by the organisation to charity are an important feature when they are making their choice of employer and the company's high profile commitment to the charity of the year has been significant in improving our ability to attract new staff, and raising the organisational pride of existing employees.

Society benefits

Benefits to society have been considerable. Each year the chosen charity of the year benefits from over £1 million, with additional funds raised going to the other short-listed charities. The funds raised through the Million £ Challenge make a significant contribution to the three short-listed charities' work.

'NSPCC/Children 1ST are indebted to HBOS for their support. The financial contribution is one of the biggest corporate donations allowing us to reach even more vulnerable children.

• 750 of the UK's most vulnerable children will be directly helped by the income generated from the campaign.

- The HBOS Foundation covered all expenditure including production of fundraising materials during the campaign.

- The ratio of staff to income is impressive.

'It has created a mutually beneficial partnership that raised a significant income for NSPCC/Children 1ST but also produced a long-term relationship that, over time, will encourage a depth and scope of work between the two organisations.

'2005 was a record-breaking year for the HBOS Foundation, which NSPCC/Children 1ST were privileged to share with them. They raised more money than ever before, engaged more staff than ever before and now hold their very own world record! The enthusiasm, energy and sheer hard work of HBOS staff is remarkable and their commitment to improving the lives of people both at home and abroad is inspiring.'

Conclusion

This is an exciting, complex, successful, innovative, unique project comprising a collaboration of all the HBOS group of companies. It achieves the objectives set for it and much more besides. The HBOS Million £ Challenge has been genuinely ground-breaking. Within the charitable community it has raised the organisation's profile and many charities have made requests to participate in a future charity of the year project.

The broad range of fundraising events and activities which take place are varied, lively and fun. They provided many opportunities for staff and stakeholder involvement and engagement.

The combination of centrally organised and local activities enables us to punctuate the year with high-profile initiatives alongside the many and varied local fundraising projects.

The project continually meets the targets set for it in terms of fundraising, cross-divisional collaboration, employee advocacy and building awareness and appreciation of the group's community investment programme.

CHAPTER SIXTEEN

United for UNICEF
A case study of a winning partnership

Beth Nicholls

Working together, Manchester United, one of the world's most widely recognised sports brands, and the United Nations Children's Fund (UNICEF), the world's largest organisation working specifically for children, are a powerful force for change. Since the partnership's establishment in 1999, over £2 million has been raised to improve the lives of more than 1.5 million children all over the globe, including in China, India, Thailand, Laos, Vietnam, South Africa, Sierra Leone, Mozambique, Afghanistan and Iraq. A staggering one billion people worldwide have been reached with key UNICEF messages thanks to the powerful voice of the players.

The partnership has evolved through several distinct stages over the past seven years. Prior to any formal relationship, Manchester United brought UNICEF in to establish that there was no child labour being used in the club's merchandise supply chain, particularly with regard to footballs sourced in India. Fortunately there were no such issues, and what began as a sharing of expertise was formalised into the United for UNICEF partnership in 1999.

Manchester United has a clear strategy for its charity and community work, with three distinct tiers of support: local, national and international. The United for UNICEF partnership is a mutually exclusive one – UNICEF is the only international charity Manchester United supports, and Manchester United is the only Premiership club UNICEF UK works with. The exclusive nature of the partnership allows the club to have a significant impact in one area, to choose strategically where to focus support, and to maximise allocation of resources.

First term (1999–2002): growing the partnership

There is an excellent fit between the two organisations, both of which are committed to investing in youth, and understand the power of sport to shape lives. In the first three years of the partnership, Manchester United supported UNICEF's education work. The club underwrote a fundraising target of £1 million which was reached by 2002, and used to fund a ground-breaking project in West Bengal, India. This saw the creation of 16,000 schools in hard-to-reach areas, giving over 1 million children the chance of a primary education.

In this early stage, we focused on fundraising, preferring to wait until we had actual programmatic results before carrying out any significant media activity to tell the story of what we had achieved together.

Second term (2002–05): shaping the partnership

Thrilled with the success of the first term, we agreed to renew the partnership for a further three years, building on the trust and respect that had grown between our two organisations over the previous three years. We succeeded in raising a further £1 million in the second term. The focus of the partnership moved from education to support of UNICEF UK's End Child Exploitation campaign, and it evolved from pure fundraising to also contributing advocacy support.

The campaign itself was launched at Old Trafford, and Manager Sir Alex Ferguson and a number of the first team players recorded public service announcements (PSAs) which served as advocacy tools for the campaign. The club also supported a major anti-trafficking pilot programme in China as part of this campaign (see 'Maximising Partnership Potential', below).

Third term (2005–09): taking stock and planning for the future

After six years of working together, Manchester United asked us to pitch for partnership renewal, against another well-known international charity wishing to become the club's sole international charity partner. This pitching process gave both UNICEF and Manchester United the opportunity to reflect on what we had achieved together, decide whether partnership extension was the right choice for each of us, and develop a clear strategy for the future. We agreed a four-year extension to take United for UNICEF to a ten-year celebration in 2009, which will make it the longest collaboration between a Premiership football club and a global charity.

The third term of the partnership has seen Manchester United spearhead UNICEF's first ever global campaign, 'Unite for Children, Unite against AIDS', a campaign aimed at putting children at the heart of the world's response to the AIDS pandemic.

Speaking at the campaign launch at the UN in Geneva, Manchester United manager Sir Alex Ferguson said,

'We recognise that AIDS is one of the biggest challenges facing mankind today. At Manchester United we know about reaching out to young people. We have many players who, we believe, are responsible as role models for the younger generation. Together we can change attitudes, perceptions and ultimately, behaviour.'

As one of the first major corporate partners to come on board with the global campaign, Manchester United demonstrated the vision, leadership and commitment that has been evident since the beginning of the partnership.

In this third term, we are extending our work together beyond the fundraising and advocacy of the first two terms, to include harnessing the club's sporting expertise to make a direct contribution to our programme work on the ground. This will focus mainly on HIV/AIDS education among the children and young people who represent the 'window of hope' for an AIDS-free generation.

As of 2006, the United for UNICEF partnership falls under the umbrella of the newly formed Manchester United Foundation.

Manager and player support

Manager Sir Alex Ferguson and players Ryan Giggs and Ole Gunnar Solskjaer are all UNICEF ambassadors in their own right, as are former United players David Beckham, Quinton Fortune and Diego Forlan. Prior to being asked to become UNICEF ambassadors, each one of them quietly demonstrated their personal commitment to UNICEF over a number of years, with field visits, campaign support, event support and donations.

In an age where celebrities are all too often used to add glamour to a cause without any real understanding of what the issues are, this long-term partnership allows time for the players and management to develop a real understanding of what is being supported, and why their contribution is so important and valuable. These sporting icons are powerful voices for communicating key messages and effecting change, ultimately improving the lives of children around the world. Public service announcements (PSAs) filmed with a number of the players in English, French, Spanish, Portugese and Chinese have covered topics as wide-ranging as girls' education, anti-trafficking, non-violence and HIV/AIDS awareness as well as fundraising appeals, and have been broadcast in over 35 countries.

Most of the ambassadors have children of their own and have spent time in the field, talking to children and young people, experiencing their day-to-day lives, and understanding what kind of issues they face. When they talk they do so based on what they have seen with their own eyes, and this genuine belief in and commitment to UNICEF shines through.

Every year Sir Alex Ferguson hosts an annual dinner at the Old Trafford stadium to raise money for the partnership, with all the first team players in attendance. Ole Gunnar Solskjaer has personally raised enough money to build a school in Eritrea, part of which was financed by the donation of his boot sponsorship. Over the course of each year, every single player supports UNICEF voluntarily in some way, whether that be with attendance at an event, or on a field visit, media interviews, a donation of merchandise or a personal contribution. This incredible commitment is the result of many years of working together and delivering tangible results.

Knock-on effects of the United for UNICEF partnership

The United for UNICEF partnership was UNICEF's first partnership in the football world, but it has paved the way for a number of other high-profile partnerships with governing bodies and other professional clubs including FIFA, CONCACAF, CONMEBOL, AC Milan, Feyenoord, and most recently Barcelona FC. It has had a knock-on effect for UNICEF's partnerships in other sports, including with the NBA, ATP, Asian Cricket Council and International Volleyball Federation. It has also been emulated by others, with Premiership clubs increasingly looking to follow Manchester United's example and contribute to communities where they have fans across the globe.

The knock-on effect has benefited UNICEF globally to the tune of many millions of pounds, and helped the organisation reach a new audience with key messages about the issues facing children today.

Global appeal

Manchester United has global appeal and one of the largest fan bases in the world, including many supporters living in developing countries. This provides an excellent resource to tap into for raising both funds and awareness. In return, the club is committed to giving back to the communities where its fans live, whether that be Bury or Bangkok, Moss Side or Maputo. The club is able to do this through the United for UNICEF partnership, thanks to UNICEF's presence in 193 countries worldwide. This was demonstrated when the Asian tsunami struck on Boxing Day 2004. On New Year's Eve, six of the first team players recorded an appeal message, and between them the players, club employees and fans donated £150,000.

A year later the head of the club's youth academy and former United star Brian McClair took Floribert Ngalula, a Manchester United youth team player, to Thailand to see how UNICEF had used funds to support the rebuilding of communities devastated by the waves. Together we made a documentary for Manchester United Television (MUTV), which enabled us to report back to the fans who had so generously donated to the appeal. On their return to the UK, Brian and Floribert also made a presentation to the young players in the Youth Academy. Manchester United is a club famed for home-grown talent and genuinely committed to developing rounded players. Brian McClair feels that the partnership is an important one. On his return from Thailand he said,

'I strongly believe that we are producing rounded individuals at United, with exposure to global issues an important part of their education. Getting involved in Manchester United's community work helps to reinforce the players' sense of perspective.'

There is a role for the United for UNICEF partnership to help keep the players grounded as their careers take off. Both Manchester United and UNICEF take this aspect of the partnership seriously, as the young players of today are the role models of tomorrow.

Partnership objectives

Together we set very clear objectives for the partnership and report on progress at bi-annual strategy meetings with the Manchester United board and Manchester United Foundation. At these meetings we also agree our activity plans for the coming months. The objectives for the third term of the partnership are:

- to raise funds and awareness for UNICEF's international work for children (further £1 million for Unite for Children, Unite against AIDS campaign by 2009)

- to advocate for children's rights

- to invest in the young

- to build brand value for both partners

- to assist Manchester United to be a socially responsible industry leader

- to harness the power of the players' voices to communicate key messages about issues facing children globally.

Having such specific objectives helps us prioritise activities as various opportunities arise, and also helps us evaluate whether the partnership has achieved what it set out to do.

Types of fundraising

United for UNICEF fundraising falls into four main categories:

1   Gala events – including an annual dinner at the stadium with all first team players in attendance
2   Football events – including a benefit game and closed season football events on the pitch at Old Trafford
3   Donations – from the club, players, employees and supporters both in the UK and overseas
4   Activities and promotions with Manchester United's sponsors and licensees.

Part of our strategy for the third term of the partnership has been to engage more with the club's sponsors and licensees. A prime example of this is the arrangement we have with Serious USA, who produce innovative PS2 and Xbox compatible DVD Cardz™ featuring individual Manchester United players. In a two-year deal, Serious donate 2p from every card sold to United for UNICEF, with a minimum guarantee of £50,000. Perhaps even more importantly, the United for UNICEF PSAs recorded by certain players are included as exclusive content on those players' DVD Cardz, and supported by information about those players' involvement in the partnership in the magazines which accompany each of the Cardz. This gives us direct access to a new young audience of fans who look up to the featured players as their role models. There is on-pack credit for the partnership, and an interactive hyperlink which drives traffic from the card directly to the United for UNICEF microsite to encourage further donations and awareness.

Another example is the 'Goals for Kids' initiative launched by Manchester United's principal sponsor, American International Group Inc. (AIG) in August 2006. The company will donate £1,000 for every goal scored by United in the 2006/7 season. Some of the funds raised by this initiative will support a United for UNICEF-funded HIV/AIDS prevention programme in Sierra Leone, with the remainder going to support local children's charities around Manchester.

Manchester United has also provided introductions to their major sponsors which have developed into stand-alone corporate partnerships with UNICEF. After seeing the value of United for UNICEF, Vodafone gave £1 million over three years to fund UNICEF's work tackling child trafficking in eastern Europe, and Western Union provided €1 million to fund early childhood development programmes.

Maximising partnership potential

With each major activity we do, we try to include three elements: fundraising; advocacy and programme; media and PR.

For example, during Manchester United's 2005 Asia tour to Hong Kong, China and Japan, we planned and carried out the following multi-layered programme of activity.

1   **Fundraising** – We engaged supporters through in-stadium competitions, a community football tournament and an auction at the tour's gala dinner.

2   **Advocacy and programme** – As part of their support for our End Child Exploitation campaign, Manchester United committed to supporting UNICEF's work with the government of China to combat the in-country trafficking of women and children. In China alone, official statistics estimate that more than 10,000 women and children are trafficked every year. Manchester United contributed over £230,000 to a pilot programme in Sichuan province with the aim of enhancing the prevention of trafficking and the rescue and rehabilitation of child and women victims. Developed by UNICEF in collaboration with government counterparts, the project has assisted the fight against trafficking in China from policy to grass roots level. The funds were spent on delivering a girls trafficking prevention training programme in 2,000 primary schools; a multi-media, multi-level communication campaign; support for the recovery and rehabilitation of trafficking victims; and policy development including a national plan of action for anti-trafficking and appropriate legislation.

To enhance this work, anti-trafficking PSAs were recorded with players Ryan Giggs (in English with subtitles) and Dong Fang Zhou (in Chinese) and broadcast across the country on Chinese state television and in the stadiums during the club's 2005 Asia tour.

3   **Media and PR** – Besides the actual broadcast of the educational PSAs featuring Giggs and Dong, the press conference held in Beijing to announce the funding of the anti-trafficking project gathered more journalists than any other press conference during the tour. It was hosted by China's ministry of commerce, and chief executive David Gill, manager Sir Alex Ferguson and players Ryan Giggs and Dong Fang Zhou and the representative for UNICEF China were joined by several young girls from Sichuan province who were benefiting from the programme. Unprecedented media coverage across China and in the UK saw Manchester United being favourably compared against Real Madrid who had recently toured the country:

139

'Real Madrid is collecting money, while Manchester United is giving out money to help children.'

Quinlong Sports

'Manchester United and Real Madrid left Chinese people with totally different impressions. Manchester United are the real winners.'

Tianjin Metro Express

This media coverage promoted Manchester United's global CSR commitment to audiences in the UK and overseas. It shows how the United for UNICEF partnership can enhance the Manchester United brand perception in one of the club's key emerging markets, impacting on existing fans, new audiences, sponsors, other stakeholders and media.

Challenges

The main challenge for a longstanding partnership like United for UNICEF is keeping it fresh. While some events can and do happen on an annual basis, many others are one-off and creativity is required to constantly come up with new ideas that will work within the club's busy football schedule. It is vital to keep all stakeholders engaged, regularly reporting back on what has been achieved and keeping them updated with what still needs to be done.

The change of campaign focus every three years has worked very well for the partnership. While the whole club remains committed to UNICEF's overall goal to make a world fit for children, the change of focus provides a new rallying point every few years. Three to four years is long enough to probe into an issue in considerable depth, but the change of focus at the end of that period enables the players, employees and fans to learn about something new.

Key factors for success

Based on the seven years of experience we have with the United for UNICEF partnership, the key factors for success can be summarised as follows.

• **Natural fit between the two partners, and genuine commitment to the cause and issues**
There is a clear fit between our two organisations, both operating on a global scale and market leaders in our respective industries, both with a passion for what we do, a focus on sport and with young people at the heart of our work.

Together we choose the issue we focus on for any given term of the partnership, and the first team players are polled to ensure they are comfortable with the issue and keen to support it.

FIGURE 16.1 KEY FACTORS FOR SUCCESS

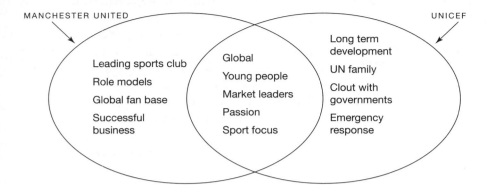

- **Clear jointly agreed partnership objectives including recognition of the corporate partner's need for measurable commercial benefits**
See 'Partnership objectives' above for details of the clear objectives we have jointly set for the partnership. UNICEF is aware of the need to demonstrate measurable commercial benefits to Manchester United (including the measurement of equivalent advertising value of media coverage) and regularly carries out market research and media evaluations around major activities.

- **Understanding of the constraints and limitations within our respective businesses**
This understanding has deepened over the course of the partnership, so we are now in a position where we appreciate what is and what is not possible, and plan accordingly. This also allows us to devise activities that are mutually beneficial, and prioritise when putting requests to the club, bearing in mind the busy football schedule the club has to work to.

- **Cross-club engagement and commitment**
The importance of support at all levels of the club, from the management and team through to the board and employees, from sponsors and club media to past players and supporters should not be underestimated. For example, to carry out and maximise effectiveness of fundraising and awareness-raising activities on a match day requires at least the support of the following: manager and players, club secretary, Kit Man, groundsman and ground staff, stadium announcer, television commentators, matchday programme and website journalist, player liaison, marketing team, Manchester United Foundation staff. Without the cooperation of all these people, partnership activities will not be successful. Different activities need the support of different people, but it is always and without exception a team effort.

- **Excellent communication and regular feedback to stakeholders**

UNICEF allocates a dedicated account manager to the partnership, who is based in Manchester. We also have a senior media officer and media officer working specifically on the account, and have a director-level project sponsor. Manchester United provide a global community liaison to work on the United for UNICEF account. This allocation of resources on both sides has proved key to the success of the partnership, and allows daily contact by phone and email, as well as weekly face-to-face working meetings at Old Trafford. We hold bi-annual strategy meetings with the Manchester United board and Foundation.

Regular feedback to stakeholders is vital to ensure ongoing support and we do this through:

- the meetings outlined above
- Manchester United Television (MUTV) documentaries, interviews and news pieces
- Manchester United Radio
- *United* magazine
- *Red Lines* (Manchester United internal magazine)
- regular features in matchday programmes
- news articles on www.manutd.com and www.unicef.org.uk
- our dedicated microsite at www.manutd.com/unitedforunicef
- local, national and international media coverage.

- **Recognising the value of the wider benefits of the partnership beyond fundraising**

The partnership needs to work on several levels, and it is important for the club to feel that they are making a valuable contribution beyond simply writing out a cheque. Indeed, if the club was engaged in fundraising alone, this would be a missed opportunity for the charity, as professional sports clubs have so much more to offer, as demonstrated in 'Maximising Partnership Potential', above.

Summary

The United for UNICEF partnership was highly commended at the UK Charity Awards in 2006. This recognised the fact that no other charity partnership in the UK exists on the scale of United for UNICEF, which marries the power of one of the world's most influential football clubs with the world's largest organisation working specifically for children. Manchester United has consistently demonstrated a pioneering approach to community involvement and their focused commitment to UNICEF. The partnership is mutually beneficial, bringing key business benefits to Manchester United whilst raising significant funds for UNICEF.

The use of high-profile football players to advocate and educate is highly innovative and to date has brought key UNICEF messages to over 1 billion people globally.

Manchester United and UNICEF have together harnessed the popularity and power of football to have a real and lasting impact on the lives of over 1.5 million children.

'The world is united through its love of football and it is this passion that enables it to have a broader impact on the lives of millions of children. Football can promote improved health and education for the world's children, prevention of HIV/AIDS and a child's right to recreation. For too many children, this and other basic benefits have not been realised. With this in mind I salute Manchester United for their support for UNICEF.'

Kofi Annan, secretary general, United Nations

'We at Manchester United greatly value the United for UNICEF partnership. I speak not only for myself but for all levels of the club including our players, employees and fans who over six years have demonstrated their support for UNICEF as our chosen international charity partner. Our investment into the futures of children and young people is a long-term commitment. We want to help UNICEF achieve their development priorities. This partnership gives us the tools to be as effective as possible in helping those children who are less fortunate than our own and we will be immensely proud to see our six years of making a difference grow into a ten-year collaboration. We all look forward lending our experience in sport to UNICEF to help enhance and support grassroots programmes for children which use sport to inspire, engage and develop children and deliver UNICEF's goals.'

David Gill, chief executive, Manchester United

CHAPTER SEVENTEEN

British Institute for Brain Injured Children (BIBIC) and IPC Media

A charity of the year partnership in the media industry

Jill Taylor and Taryn Barclay

BIBIC and corporate fundraising

BIBIC is a national children's charity established in 1972. Historically the income stream from corporates has been very modest, usually much less than 10 per cent of the fundraising income and in some years as low as 5 per cent, none of which came from major companies.

A 10-year strategic plan identified corporate partnerships as worthy of continued effort despite the evidence that whenever BIBIC had been selected as a worthy cause to go forward to a large employee or customer vote, it would lose out to the well known charities with high brand recognition.

In a small to medium-sized charity with a limited budget, the question is not only of recruiting and retaining high-calibre fundraisers, but also one of opportunity cost. If it was decided to employ a dedicated fundraiser to a specific target segment, would it pay dividends or would we be better spending the money on a fundraiser directed to a different area of income generation? This is a tricky thing to argue for a corporate fundraiser when your profile isn't large, but after several interviewing sessions, and an agreement not to accept candidates that 'might do', we employed someone who definitely 'could do', who added to our intellectual capital by being able to craft high quality corporate and media partner applications. The temptation again was to focus on steady money – five hundred pounds here, a thousand there – but we kept a steady hand, decided to focus on charity of the year partnerships and accepted that there would be a time lag despite the financial pressures of doing so.

BIBIC had not considered that one of the first major partnerships would be with a company the size of IPC Media.

IPC Media's first charity of the year

IPC Media is the UK's leading consumer magazine publisher, with an unrivalled portfolio of brands, selling over 350 million copies each year. Its magazines reach over 70 per cent of UK women and 50 per cent of UK men, which is over 28 million UK adults. IPC's diverse portfolio includes *What's on TV, Now, Marie Claire, In Style, Woman & Home, Ideal Home, NME, Wallpaper*, Country Life, The Field, Rugby World, Practical Boat Owner, Pick Me Up, TV easy* – the list goes on.

Over the previous two years, IPC Media had been striving to create and implement a corporate responsibility (CR) strategy, focusing on three main areas: community initiatives, environmental management and employee engagement. The IPC Media charity of the year programme formed a key part of employee engagement, as the main objective behind this initiative was to support the community efforts of IPC Media employees. This was realised by making the successful charity of the year an organisation already supported by an employee.

The programme also involved employees in the final selection process, so as to create greater support for the fundraising activities that would be part of the programme. It was also felt to be crucial to involve staff in the whole process as IPC Media wanted this to be an initiative that would enable employees to relate to the overall CR work of IPC Media and not just the specific charity partnerships that already exist with the individual magazines. Part of the corporate challenge is to create meaningful connections for people to IPC Media as many staff tend to see themselves as employees of, for example, *NME* or *Country Life*, rather than IPC Media, such is the strength of the brand affiliation for many employees. Although largely based in London, IPC Media does have magazine offices in other locations, which adds to this challenge.

The process for selecting the charity that would become the recipient of IPC's fundraising and awareness-raising activities over the designated period, was to first establish a selection committee that would be responsible for shortlisting organisations nominated by employees. The committee was made up of two IPC Media main board directors, two staff council members, the CR manager, the director of corporate communications and an HR representative. Crucial to the selection process were the criteria that the committee would need to apply to each nomination, so as to ensure that the final organisation met all the requirements of this programme. The selection criteria are listed below.

1   Personal involvement – applicants must be able to demonstrate direct involvement in the organisation, either through volunteering, fundraising or being a member of the board/trustees committee. This excludes one-off fundraising through charity runs or walks.

2   The nominated organisation must have an annual revenue of not more than £10 million and financial income statements must be provided with the application. The organisation must also be able to demonstrate its main sources of funding.

3   Community focused – the organisation would need to demonstrate how it contributes to improvements of the communities it supports. The organisation may do this either locally or through a wide network of locations. The charity could be the local branch of a national organisation but does not necessarily need to be affiliated to a national charity/community organisation.

4   Registered charitable status – the organisation must be a registered charity as defined by the Charity Commission.

The following organisations were not eligible to apply for this programme: trade unions; alumni organisations; political campaigns, parties, candidates of parties; and organisations that discriminate against others on the basis of race, creed, religion, ethnicity, nationality, gender or sexual orientation.

The application process was fairly formal, with employees having to complete an official application form that asked for specific details relating to both their involvement with the charity or community organisation and an outline of the work that this organisation does in the community. The selection committee then applied the criteria to each nomination and finally decided on a shortlist of three charities. Each charity was then invited to give a presentation on its work and how a partnership with IPC could help. This assessment process included a visit attended by members of the selection committee. The visit and presentation enabled the committee to have first-hand experience of the charity's work and also allowed for verification of the criteria and information presented on the application form.

The three charities were next invited to set up a stand at an open day to talk to interested employees in their breaks. IPC employees then voted for their preferred charity through the company's internal communications channels, namely the daily electronic newsletter (*Inbrief*) and the company intranet.

It is planned that fundraising activities will take place on two levels. The first is staff focused, encouraging staff to participate in organised events for BIBIC as well as creating internal opportunities to donate to the charity. A major focus will be to work on increasing payroll giving as a way to encourage longer-term giving. Internal fundraising has already received some help this year from IPC Media at a corporate level, with a donation from the company's e-Christmas card and the company agreeing to donate the per-head cost of the annual Christmas lunch to BIBIC on behalf of those employees who decide to donate their voucher instead of taking up their lunch.

The other exciting area of fundraising is leveraging the power of IPC Media's magazines by drawing readers' attention to BIBIC (as appropriate to the magazine's editorial style). For example, an annual feature in the December issue of *InStyle* is the Christmas giveaway competition and associated editorial. In the past the editor would select a charity as their own choice of beneficiary, but this year, due to the employee launch of the initiative, the editor selected BIBIC. All the proceeds from the premium-rate telephone number will be donated to BIBIC, which clearly illustrates the magazines lending their support with a direct financial impact.

Although IPC does not dictate editorial content at a corporate level, the partnership with BIBIC is a door-opener to raise awareness among editorial teams. Introducing BIBIC to those who may be able to feature BIBIC's work in the magazines is a key objective for the partnership. This will expand the charity of the year programme to focus not solely on internal fundraising, as IPC Media as a company is able to lend considerable media exposure to the charity. This was also one of the key reasons that IPC wanted to work with a smaller and lesser known charity to really make a tangible difference during the partnership period.

Benefits for BIBIC

BIBIC values the efforts involved in the employee fundraising activities. The income that it will bring during the 15-month partnership will make a valuable financial contribution to being able to deliver the charity's core aims. But the benefit of the media exposure is recognised as having the possibility of making a step-change for the charity in the coming year. The partnership in its entirety will not only bring in further income but also publicise the charity, raise profile and allow more new families to access our services, which will fulfil our mission. In some charities even of BIBIC's size, communications and fundraising can have their own separate paths, a media partnership enables maximum benefit and ensures the two are inextricably linked.

As is noted elsewhere in this book, it is not only the cash donations that are valuable, it is the potential for a really creative partnership. We all know the power of the media and its ability to take a message to a wide audience. BIBIC have families who are willing to put themselves in the spotlight to highlight the work of the charity so that others will hear of, and have an opportunity to access, the service.

While it might be obvious that a charity such as BIBIC could be proactive in presenting family case studies to women's magazines, the challenge is to offer different angles to different magazines. Lateral thinking generates ideas, for example, BIBIC promotes the value of good nutrition and if possible an organic diet as part of a holistic therapy programme, and this might be an angle to engage the editors of gardening and home-lifestyle publications. Likewise, an understanding of sensory environments, either more stimulating or less stimulating depending on a child's condition, could be the subject of a makeover article in a women's magazine. With IPC's vast array of titles, the challenge is for the charity to be proactive wherever possible.

With so many families being supported nationwide there are a number who are willing to give their permission for their story to be told so as to provide a story 'exclusive' to each title. One of BIBIC's trustees is a grandmother of a child on programme, and she and her daughter, the child's mother, are willing to be featured in *Woman's Weekly* for the charity's benefit. Good communications about the practical work undertaken will also drive donations and the possibility of further fundraising doors being opened.

One of the strengths of working for a charity of BIBIC's size is that the combination of dynamic people and opportunity can potentially alter the fortunes of a charity: this is the case with the opportunity given by the IPC Media partnership. The corporate communications department at IPC Media have been discussing with individual editors how they might help. As a result it was agreed that *Woman* would place a pro bono insert in its pre-Christmas edition. A downside of working for a charity of BIBIC's size is resources, or lack of them. What did BIBIC have as a suitable insert? Nothing of note! The result was a newly designed leaflet which was created with a regular-giving ask mechanism, proofed, printed and delivered in three weeks flat.

In some charities there can be internal tension between communications and fundraising departments when working with a media partner. In BIBIC the two functions are combined. The insert, although essentially a fundraising device, therefore also carried a strong message that if the recipient was aware of any family needing help, they should contact BIBIC.

This partnership has brought benefits to other fundraising income streams and enabled BIBIC to carry out work we had identified as important, but had not been able to fund. For example, the plan had identified that it would be desirable to test-market a direct mail campaign, but the cost of outsourcing this was more than could be justified to invest in the acquisition of new donors. Also existing regular donors were signed up via standing orders, as there were not enough givers to warrant setting up a direct debit originator system. The opportunity to include 500,000 inserts asking for regular donations in *Woman* magazine moved the question of direct debits from being 'something we had in mind' to working with Barclays Bank to turn round our application to open an account in eight days rather than eight weeks, in order to include include it on the leaflet. Outsourcing was considered, but it was felt that there was the internal capacity to deal with the account's administration. Had time allowed, the design would have been tested for the target audience. The ROI (return on investment) is yet to be evaluated. For additional opportunities it may be possible to link in with IPC Media's online focus groups to give an opinion on the likely impact.

In recent years, the charity has not been successful in, or invested a great deal of effort into, attracting celebrity support, but the opportunity to be introduced to celebrities is heightened because a number write for IPC Media's magazines.

Because of the charity's mission, BIBIC's fundraisers are aware that in any audience they address it is highly likely that there will be families that need the type of specialist support BIBIC provides. Therefore among employees' families at IPC Media there will be those who have children with a condition such as Down's syndrome, autism, asperger's syndrome, cerebral palsy, an acquired or genetic brain injury, ADHD, dyslexia or dyspraxia. Internal communication through the charity of the year selection process, on the company's intranet, and in the employee magazine has raised interest in the work of the charity. As a result, an initial meeting to explore the possibility of establishing an employee disability support group has been arranged. This initiative moves the relationship from the fundraising to the family services department at BIBIC and from the corporate affairs department to the support of the HR department. It is intended that BIBIC will provide behavioural management strategies, tips and advice and training in disability awareness to the group. This may become linked back into profile-raising for BIBIC creating a better understanding of issues that can be reported on for Brain Injury Awareness Week, which has its annual focus in March.

As a charity with a national geographical reach of clients, it was recognised by the board of trustees that this was not the case in the make-up of the members and needed to be addressed. The corporate communications team at IPC Media were asked if with the company's contacts they would be able to suggest any potential trustees so as to broaden the skills and expertise within the organisation.

As corporate fundraisers are aware, the ingredients for a charity of the year should bring the full spectrum of charitable giving, time, money and goods. A media partnership of the scale of IPC Media is certainly doing just that for BIBIC.

IPC Media's evaluation

Since the partnership has only been in place for four months, it is early days in terms of evaluation and learning. There have, however, already been events which have not had the desired response. For example, BIBIC organises a Cue Sport Marathon, a national campaign that runs annually in October and November. Having a fairly young workforce and a very social culture, it was assumed that this would be a popular event for IPC staff to participate in. The response was completely the opposite and it was difficult to understand the reasons why there was such a poor response. A potential learning from this is that IPC staff may be more inclined to participate in something that is already happening or that they can indirectly support – for example, the sale of Christmas cards or the donation of the Christmas lunch voucher were well supported. Staff ordinarily buy cards, so they could now buy BIBIC cards; a group of employees don't normally eat in the company canteen, so donating their company lunch voucher was an easy thing to do.

The key ingredient seems to be that the events or activities must tap into an existing motivation or habit or something that is an 'easy give'. Some of the ideas for fundraising for 2007 include requesting donations from the magazines in terms of their own expertise, contacts or skills – this is about harnessing what the magazine teams already have in their possession and which will be easy for them to donate or participate in. Furthermore, being in such a creative environment, it is hoped that staff will start having their own ideas about events. There have already been several ideas and activities initiated and proposed by staff themselves, and with great results.

Future plans

The charity of the year partnership is a key part of IPC's employee engagement strategy, so it is essential that IPC employees are motivated and enthused to get involved with events for BIBIC.

Having such a diverse group of employees does provide challenges, but at the same time each group has something to offer. Already a significant sum of money has been raised and there has been high-profile editorial coverage of BIBIC in three of IPC Media's most successful and high-circulation magazines.

The programme of activity for the following 12 months is to grow the level of involvement of staff

● to encourage them to propose their own fundraising ideas,

● to continue seeking out opportunities for awareness raising for the charity

● to help BIBIC meet their own strategic objectives that will fulfil their own goals, long after the partnership has ended.

PART 3
Appendices

Legal and tax issues

Anne-Marie Piper

This appendix chapter covers the legal and tax issues (as at January 2007) associated with corporate fundraising.

In recent years, businesses have become an increasingly important source of cash and other much needed resources for charities. However, as other chapters in this book has shown, corporate fundraising today extends far beyond pure philanthropy into the realms of business development and promotion and includes:

- donations

- companies with 'in-house' charities

- payroll giving

- matched giving schemes (when employers add to donation/fundraising by their staff)

- gift-in-kind, including secondments

- commercial participation

- brand licensing

- sponsorship.

However, before examining the charity law and tax rules relating to these methods, it will be helpful to take a step back to look at the legal framework charities must operate within when dealing with their corporate partners. This framework includes:

- the duties of charity trustees

- subsidiary trading companies

- the difference between donations and other arrangements

- different types of corporate supporters

- negotiations (including confidentiality agreements)

- contracts and lawyers
- using professional fundraisers
- substantial donors.

Health warning

As this appendix will show, the legal and fiscal consequences of arrangements between charities and their corporate supporters can vary hugely depending on the way they are structured. This appendix should not be read as a comprehensive analysis of its subject matter – it is designed only to give its readers a very brief and general overview of the subject so that they are familiar with the general landscape, know some of the more important questions to ask and, perhaps most importantly, when they should be seeking help.

The legal framework

The duties of charity trustees

The decision to accept a gift from or to enter into an arrangement with a corporate supporter is one which, in law, ultimately vests with the charity trustees of the charity.

Who are the trustees?

Under charity law the 'charity trustees' of a charity are the people who have ultimate responsibility and control over the management of the charity. With charitable trusts, the trustees are likely to be called trustees (although this is not always the case); however, with charitable companies and other forms of charities, the trustees may be called directors, members of the board of trustees, members of the council of management or the executive committee. The name given to them doesn't matter, nor does it matter how they got to be trustees – they might have been elected, nominated, appointed, ex officio (serve by virtue of occupying some other post or office) – their duties are the same.

Delegated authority/responsibility

In many charities it would be impossible for the trustees to take all the decisions involved with the running of the charity and so much decision-making will be delegated to staff and/or sub-committees.

When exercising delegated authority, staff and/or sub-committees need to have regard to the responsibilities of the trustees. The trustees and those to whom they delegate also need to be clear about the extent of the authority that is to be delegated. Is the chief executive/sub-committee's brief simply to negotiate the best deal they can for the trustees to approve? Or, have they been authorised by the trustees to conclude an arrangement and, if so, are they aware of how documents need to be signed on behalf of the charity?

Trustees need to be clear about the extent of any authority they delegate (or don't delegate) not only because they will usually remain responsible for decisions taken by their delegates but also because they may be responsible for some decisions that they have not delegated, thanks to the legal doctrine of ostensible authority. Very briefly, if it is reasonable for a person to believe that someone they are dealing with has authority to enter into the arrangement they have negotiated, then, whether or not that person actually has the authority, they will be treated as having it.

Trustees' duties: an overview

Charity trustees have an overriding duty to act in the best interests of their charity. This principle is easily stated but more difficult to apply in practice.

Within the duty to act in the best interests of the charity are a number of subsidiary duties which include the duty:

• to apply the assets of the charity only for the charitable purposes within charity's objects

• to maximise and protect the assets of the charity

• to exercise proper stewardship and to run the charity in accordance with its constitution and the law

• to avoid, or deal appropriately with, conflicts of interest

• to take advice from appropriately qualified persons on areas beyond the expertise of the trustees or staff of the charity.

The duty to apply the assets of the charity only for the charitable purposes within the charity's objects

This requirement precludes trustees from benefiting or subsidising commercial organisations (even the charity's wholly owned subsidiary trading companies) or indeed charities or not-for-profit organisations whose activities are outside the charity's objects.

In practice this means that it is important for trustees and their corporate fundraisers to look critically at arrangements with a corporate partner if the arrangement involves the company benefiting in some way. A benefit given as part of a corporate sponsorship deal routed through a subsidiary trading company may be fine, but a thank-you gift by a charity grateful for a donation would probably not be lawful. This subject is explored further below in the sections relating to donations, sponsorship and the use of subsidiary trading companies.

The duty to maximise and protect the assets of the charity

Many involved with charities often overlook the fact that the charity's good name may also be its most valuable asset. Accepting a large corporate donation may not be in the best interest of the charity if, when the news gets out, it damages the reputation of the charity, causing the charity's supporters to desert it in droves.

Similarly, a sponsorship deal which requires a lot of work on the part of the charity's staff may deflect them from other work. Such a deal may not be in the best interests of the charity if the diversion could result in damage to the charity, such as losing a valuable contract.

Another aspect of this rule is that charities should seek to minimise their exposure to tax. In the case of trading activities (including sponsorship) this is often achieved by using a subsidiary trading company (see the section on the use of such companies below).

The duty to run the charity in accordance with its constitution and the law

Charities contemplating any corporate fundraising initiative need to check their constitutions to see that they have the powers they need for the proposed arrangements. Acting beyond their powers may be a breach of trust for which the trustees could be personally liable if things go wrong.

If a charity lacks the powers necessary for a particular arrangement, it may be possible to amend the constitution to remedy the situation, but this is likely to delay matters and may need the prior consent of the Charity Commission.

Charities also need to look beyond charity law when fundraising to ensure that they comply with any other laws, regulation and best practice that may apply. It is impossible to give a comprehensive list of these – they could be anything from health and safety rules to advertising codes of practice.

The duty to avoid, or deal appropriately with, conflicts of interest

Many charities are able to forge relationships with companies connected with their trustees. There is nothing wrong with such relationships but the trustees need to ensure that they are appropriately managed to ensure that the charity, the company and/or the trustee are not compromised in the process. Experience has shown that potential and perceived conflicts of interest can be as damaging as the real thing.

Good practice in this area is to ensure that the trustee concerned is distanced from the deal making and approval process (at the very least, by abstaining from any vote to approve the proposed arrangement).

The duty to take proper advice

Under charity law, charity trustees have a duty to take advice from someone suitably qualified in relation to their plans and, unless there is a good reason to the contrary, to follow that advice.

If they are lucky enough to have staff or trustees with the necessary expertise, charities can satisfy this duty in this way. However, many types of corporate fundraising will require specialist commercial, tax and other advice and the cost of this and the time it will take to get the advice must be factored into their plans.

Charities should not lightly ignore this duty or any professional advice they receive. If things go wrong and it transpires that the charity was advised against a plan or scheme, the charity's trustees leave themselves vulnerable. If faced with unwelcome professional advice, it is always wise for charities to seek a second opinion.

Trading and the use of subsidiary trading companies

The term 'subsidiary trading company' is used, in this appendix, to refer to a commercial trading company all of whose shares are owned by the 'parent' charity or charities.

To understand the need for a subsidiary trading company, it is necessary to look briefly at the basic charity law and tax rules that apply to trading and, indeed, what activities amount to trading.

What amounts to trading?

Unfortunately there is no clear statutory definition of what constitutes 'trading'. Manufacturing goods to sell is clearly trading but, less obviously, so are many corporate sponsorship deals (because the charity is, in effect, selling the company the opportunity to advertise itself or its products).

The profit motive, while important, is only one of the factors that might indicate trading. A better rule of thumb is, 'Are we providing goods or services on a commercial or semi-commercial basis?'

Charity law

As a matter of charity law, trading by charities is permissible only if it is either in pursuance of the primary purposes (known as 'primary purpose trading') or objects of the charity or of it is temporary or incidental to those purposes.

In order to ascertain whether a charity is trading in furtherance of its objects, it is essential to examine the charity's constitution. The question should then be asked, 'Does the trading activity directly further one of the charity's objects?' If it does, then it is probably primary purpose trading. Classic examples of primary purpose trading include the provisions of education at independent schools in return for fees and the sale of tickets to an exhibition by an art gallery or museum.

It is common for charity constitutions to contain a prohibition against 'permanent trading activities'. In practice the term means any trading activity which is not:

- primary purpose trading;

- trading which is either temporary or incidental to the primary purposes of the charity; or

- the sale of donated goods.

Tax

The trading profits or surpluses of a charity are generally only exempt from tax (corporation tax in the case of corporate charities; income tax in the case of unincorporated charities) if all the profits of the trade are applied solely for the charitable purposes of the charity and the trade is exercised in the course of carrying out the primary purposes of the charity.

There are a limited number of exceptions to this general rule including:

BENEFICIARY TRADING

This exemption covers non-primary purpose trading which is mainly carried out by the beneficiaries of the charity (such as the sale of goods they have made).

MIXED TRADING

Where a trading activity is partly carried out partly for charitable purposes and partly for non-primary purposes (such as a museum shop selling art-related articles and other items such as pencils and mugs), then, following changes made in 2006, HM Revenue and Customs (HMRC) will generally treat the activity as two trades, and receipts and expenses will be apportioned between the two trades. Tax will be payable on the profits of the non-primary purpose trade unless it falls within an exemption such as the small trading exemption (see below).

SMALL TRADING EXEMPTION

Charities can carry out tax-free non-primary purpose trading, as long as the income from that trade is to be within the limits allowed by law. The limits are as follows:

Charity's total gross income from all sources	Maximum turnover from non-primary purpose trade allowed
– under £20,000	– £5,000
– £20,000 – £200,000	– 25% of the charity's total gross income
– over £200,000	– £50,000

Even if turnover from non-primary is over these limits, HMRC may not tax the profits if the charity can show that it reasonably expected turnover to fall within the limits: the charity may have traded more than anticipated, or it may have received less income from other sources than it expected.

These exemptions are not blanket exemptions. Their benefit can, for example, be reduced or eliminated if a charity incurs 'non-qualifying expenditure' and so charities planning to trade – even in a modest way – need to take care and professional advice before doing so. A good starting point for charities with only a modest budget for professional help is the HMRC website.[13]

VAT

Charities do not enjoy any special exemptions from VAT because of their charitable status. This means that if charities supply goods or services for consideration (payment in money or in kind), they are in the same VAT position as a commercial organisation and they will need to be registered for VAT if their supplies exceeds the VAT threshold.

Generally, the supply of goods and services by charities will be subject to the standard rate of VAT. However, some supplies are liable to the reduced rate, the zero rate or are VAT exempt. Many charities get into difficulties by overlooking VAT (which can come back to haunt them). Again, care and professional advice are recommended and help is available on the HMRC website.

13 www.gov.uk/charities/guidance-notes/

Using a subsidiary trading company

By having a subsidiary trading company, a charity can avoid the charity law and tax pitfalls outlined above: non-primary purpose trading can be routed through the company to avoid breaches of charity law and although trading companies are liable to tax on their profits, the tax liability can be avoided by the company transferring its profits to its parent charity under the Gift Aid scheme.

Before setting up a subsidiary trading company, it is necessary to check the charity's constitution to ensure that it contains a power to form companies (or failing that a general 'do all other lawful things to promote the objects' type power). A charity which does not have a power to form a trading company will need to consider amending its constitution (which may require the prior consent of the Charity Commission).

The principle that charity funds may only be expended for charitable purposes prohibits charities from subsidising their wholly owned trading companies. The relationship between charities and their trading companies must be at arm's length. Practical considerations include:

- **The board of directors of the trading company** – The board or committee of trustees of the charity and the board of directors of the trading company should not be made up of the same people. However, it is a good idea for the trustees to be represented on the board of the company (so they are aware of what the company is doing). Trustees who are also directors of the trading company cannot usually be paid directors' fees, a salary or other benefits by the trading company (although directors who are not also trustees may receive such benefits).

- **Providing services to the trading company** – The trading company should pay for any services provided by the charity (including the use of its name and premises) and the arrangements should be recorded in a formal agreement between the two. VAT may also be chargeable on these services, so consideration should be given to forming a VAT group.

- **Financing the company** – One of the great difficulties faced by charities wishing to use subsidiary trading companies is financing them. A charity should not invest in shares in the trading company unless the trustees are satisfied, after having taken appropriate advice: that they have the power to make the investment; that the investment is both appropriate and prudent; and that the investment will qualify for tax relief. As there are almost always better investments to be made, only rarely will charities be able to justify an investment. More usually, they need to finance their trading subsidiaries by means of loans. If a charity wishes to lend money to a subsidiary, it will need to do so on fully commercial terms (including provision for its repayment, interest and security) and then only if they are satisfied that the loan will qualify for tax reliefs (to avoid falling foul of the non-qualifying expenditure and loans rules, on which guidance can be found on the HRMC website).

• **Conflicts of interest** – Trustees of a charity who are also directors of its trading company need to be aware of the different duties attaching to, and the potential for conflicts of interest arising from, their two roles. They should abstain from voting – on both boards – on arrangements between the charity and the company.

There are no charity law restrictions on benefits being passed from a trading company to its parent charity (although there are various company law provisions which may need to be considered).

The difference between donations and other arrangements

A donation is a gift for which the donor (the person making the gift) neither asks for nor receives a benefit. It is often said that a donation must be 'pure bounty' in the hands of the charity.

A donation by a company/business to charity is generally deductible (see 'Donations', below).

A donation may sometimes be subject to a condition, for example, that the gift be used towards a particular project of the charity. Such a condition will not generally affect its status (or tax treatment) as a donation. However, if a condition is one which confers a benefit on the donor or is subject to repayment in certain circumstances, the legal and tax treatment of the gift may change. For example, if a company makes a donation to a charity in connection with the publication of a research report on the condition that its logo appears prominently on the cover of the report and that its donation is mentioned in all publicity relating to the report, this may make the activity trading by the charity – the sale of advertising by the charity to the company. In such a situation the company would be advised to split the gift between an outright gift to the charity and an arrangement with the charity's trading company for the promotional element. The latter should also be tax deductible for the company, provided that it is accepted that the cost of the promotional deal is wholly and exclusively for the purpose of the business.

As a rule of thumb, charities and companies should take care and/or advice if the donor is to receive anything much more than a simple thank-you in, say, the charity's annual report.

Different types of corporate supporters

The term 'corporate' is used by fundraisers loosely to describe business donors or supporters. However, such supporters come in a variety of guises.

Companies

The vast majority of businesses will be limited liability companies – either public companies (those listed on the stock exchange) or private companies (those not so listed). In both cases the company will be run by a board of directors, owned by its shareholders and liable to pay corporation tax on its profits. A 'close company' is one with five or fewer participants.

In the eyes of the law companies are separate and distinct from their shareholders and so their boards are able to make gifts and enter into commercial arrangements in the name of the company.

A company makes Gift Aid donations simply by deducting the amount of the gift from its pre-tax profits. It does not need to make a Gift Aid declaration.

Companies are required, by law, to have key facts about them (including their full name, company number and registered address) on their notepaper, etc. which makes paperwork simpler. Companies House maintains a register of companies and this can be searched via their website www.companieshouse.gov.uk

Partnerships

Many professional practices, such as lawyers and accountants, are established not as companies, but as partnerships.

In a partnership each partner is personally liable for tax on his or her share of the profits of the business (rather than the business as a whole being liable, as in the case of companies). This can make donations from partnerships fiddly. First, unless the partnership specifies otherwise, the gift will be apportioned equally amongst the partners with each being treated as having made a personal gift of his or her share. Second, unless the partnership deed or some other document grants authority to one of the partners to sign a Gift Aid declaration on behalf of them, it will be necessary for the charity to go through the Gift Aid procedures and paperwork for each partner.

In practice many partnerships either make no 'partnership' gifts as such (leaving partners to make their own gifts as and when they think appropriate) or do so through an in-house charity.

Commercial arrangements with partnerships will often be concluded by a managing partner or chief executive with delegated authority from the partners.

There is no central or searchable register of partnerships.

Limited liability partnerships (LLPs) are partnerships that benefit from limited liability status. However, for tax purposes, they are treated in the same way as other partnerships.

Sole traders

Many people starting out in business do so without forming a company or a partnership, by simply adopting a trading name.

When a charity is dealing with such a business it can effectively ignore the trading persona – it is dealing with the individual behind the business, who will need to make donations and/or enter into commercial arrangements in his or her own name. So, if a sole trader wants to make a Gift Aid donation, the individual behind the business will need to make a Gift Aid declaration.

There is no central register of sole traders and their trading names.

Negotiating with corporates

The relationships between charities and their corporate supporters are like all relationships – some run smoothly and others less so!

For small or medium-sized charities desperate for funds, the biggest issue in the negotiations is likely to be the actual or perceived inequality of bargaining power and resources. Some companies have sophisticated corporate social responsibility departments and model charity contracts, both of which can be daunting.

This inequality of bargaining power can also lead to a number of problems for charities, including selling their association and/or services too cheaply and/or going further than they would like to appease a corporate (misguidedly adopting the attitude that 'he who pays the piper, calls the tune').

As with everything else in life, it is always a good idea for a fundraiser to do his or her homework when negotiating with a corporate:

- look at their website, recent annual reports, etc. to see what they say about themselves and their CSR policy;

- if possible, get in touch with charities that have been involved with them to hear about their experiences;

- again, if possible, look around at the deals that other charities are doing with corporate supporters.

Also:

- Do take any professional advice you need early in the negotiating process so as to avoid misunderstandings and/or impossible expectations later.

- Don't assume that the people you are dealing with (or those to whom they report) understand charities or the legal and tax framework within which they operate.

Contracts and lawyers

Many people are intimidated by the thought of contracts – they shouldn't be. Contracts are just a record of the agreement reached between two or more parties.

Although lawyers often use standard forms of contracts with lots of well tried and tested 'boiler-plate' provisions (legal jargon for the standard clauses such as notices and governing law), there is no magic to contracts. They can be a simple exchange of letters or a more formal (and usually much longer) document.

For complex deals sometimes 'heads of agreement' are used. Generally these are simply a non-binding statement setting out the main parts of the agreement that will be expanded later into a formal contract. However, sometimes they are binding and the first part of a larger multi-part arrangement. Heads of agreement should always specify whether (and if so, which of) their provisions are to be legally binding.

If what you are doing is sensitive or innovative, you may regard confidentiality and/or exclusivity as important. If this is the case, then consider entering into a preliminary but binding agreement to secure that confidentiality and/or exclusivity for the period of the negotiation.

The most important things about contracts are:

- that they record all the points agreed

- they are clear and unambiguous

- they anticipate things that will happen in the future which can be anticipated

- they include a mechanism for resolving problems and disputes (for the day if and/or when things go wrong or, at least, not according to plan)

- the parties only undertake to do things that they are actually able to do.

Many charities are unconvinced about the need for formal contracts. However, this is rarely the case if they have experienced a deal which has gone wrong and the trustees are unable to prove what was agreed, let alone finance a legal challenge against the defaulting party. The duty of proper management of the charity means that there should be a signed record or contract of all significant arrangements. However, charities can be proportionate here – if the matter is very small and following a well established pattern, the absence of a comprehensive signed record may not be crucial. On the other hand, if the charity is investing its reputation and/or a large amount of resources (cash or staff time), then a contract is a must.

All lawyers are trained to write contracts, but using a lawyer doesn't guarantee that a charity will get a good contract. There can be any number of reasons for this, including the contract being outside the lawyer's area of expertise, the lawyer not understanding the project well enough to ensure that likely outcomes are anticipated, and/or the corporate partner refusing to budge from its standard contract.

Lawyers, even small high street firms, are expensive, but there is much that a charity can do to improve the quality of a contract without necessarily paying a fortune. It always helps, both on quality and cost, if the charity puts down on paper in plain, layman's English what the deal is about, what the parties have agreed to do and when, what might go wrong and what really, really matters to them (there is little point running up a large bill for lawyers to negotiate a point which isn't very important). A layman's analysis like this is a good way of focussing both the charity and its lawyer.

It is also worth considering seeking help on a pro bono (free) basis. When a charity has a constitutional issue (such as amending its constitution or merging with another charity) it will always be best to instruct a charity law specialist. However, many contracts which fall within the title 'corporate fundraising' are commercial contracts of the kind that most commercial lawyers (perhaps with a little help from the charity's charity lawyers) can handle. Many large commercial law firms run pro bono schemes for just this situation. Such schemes are particularly beneficial if the corporate with which the charity is dealing is a large, well financed one with an in-house legal team (who may be wedded to their standard contracts) used to dealing with and respecting the views of the big legal hitters.

If the charity is able to secure pro bono help, make sure that the terms of the arrangement are clear. There is a world of difference between a friendly lawyer doing you a favour if and when his or her workload/life allows and a formal pro bono scheme which, to all intents and purposes, is just like using a paid lawyer, only without the bill.

Like so much in life, contracts benefit from careful attention to detail. Make sure that the trustee or fundraiser charged with negotiating the contract has the time, skill and attention to detail to do the job properly. It is also important that those responsible for approving the contract understand it. Many good people have signed contracts containing an obligation to use 'best endeavours' without realising that this was the highest standard of obligation (requiring the party to do anything and everything to achieve the stated outcome) when the other party would have settled for a 'reasonable endeavours' clause (a much lower standard).

Using professional fundraisers

A charity wishing to engage and pay a professional fundraiser to fundraise on its behalf should, by law, have a written contract with the professional fundraiser specifying:

- the name and address of each of the parties

- the date on which it was signed by or on behalf of each of them

- the period for which the agreement is to last

- any provisions for it to be terminated early

- any provisions relating to it being varied during the period of the agreement

- the principal objectives of the campaign or project for which the fundraiser is engaged, the methods to be used by the fundraiser and the charity in pursuit of those objectives

- the remuneration and expenses the fundraiser is to receive (or the method of calculating them).

In the contract the charity should also ensure that the fundraiser is obliged to comply with fundraising law and best practice (such as the Institute of Fundraising's Codes of Good Practice in Fundraising) when raising funds on its behalf.

Among the legal obligations professional fundraisers must comply with is the requirement, if they are actually approaching potential donors for funds, that they make a 'solicitation statement' in accordance with the Charities Act 1992 (a statement that specifies the charity or charities for which funds are being raised; if there is more than one charity, the basis on which they will split the funds raised; and 'in general terms' the method by which their remuneration in connection with the appeal is to be calculated).

When section 67 of the Charities Act 2006 is brought into force (probably late 2007):

- Employed fundraisers and others (such as trustees) connected with the charity who are paid for fundraising will be obliged to make a solicitation statement when approaching potential donors for funds. The content of these statements will vary slightly, but broadly it will need to clarify the collector's position within the charity and the fact that they are being paid.

● The nature of the required solicitation statement will also change so that professional fundraisers will need to specify how their remuneration is to be determined and the 'notifiable amount' (the actual amount if this is known or an estimate if it is not).

Guidance will be issued (by the Cabinet Office or the Charity Commission) on the new solicitation statement regime when section 67 is brought into force.

Substantial donors

The Finance Act 2006 introduced new rules, designed to clamp down on people and companies abusing charity tax reliefs.

Under the substantial donor rules, if a charity enters into certain transactions with a substantial donor, it will lose some of its tax reliefs.

Broadly speaking, a substantial donor is anyone (including a company) who:

● makes gifts on which it can claim charity tax reliefs (referred to as 'relievable gifts' in the Finance Act 2006) of at least £25,000 in a year, or

● makes relievable gifts of at least £100,000 in a six-year period.

Once a substantial donor has made relievable gifts of £25,000 or more in a year, they continue to be a substantial donor for the following five years.

The transactions covered are:

● a lease of property by a charity to a substantial donor or a person (or vice versa)

● the provision of services by a charity to a substantial donor (and vice versa)

● an exchange of property between a charity and a substantial donor

● the provision of financial assistance by a charity to a substantial donor (and vice versa)

● investment by the charity in a substantial donor's business

● remuneration of a substantial donor.

The charity will similarly lose tax reliefs if it enters into any of these transactions with a substantial donor or a person 'connected' to them. In the case of companies, this includes companies that are under more or less the same control as the substantial donor. In the case of substantial donors who are sole traders and partnerships, it includes family members of the sole trader/individual partners.

There are exceptions. For instance, a charity will not lose tax reliefs if it takes a lease of property from a substantial donor, if the substantial donor's business includes property letting and the terms of the lease are at least as good as those the charity could have got on the open market. It is also acceptable for a charity to invest in a substantial donor's business, if that business is a listed company.

These rules, which are likely to have a major impact on fundraising charities, are complex and at the time of writing, not the subject of any detailed HMRC guidance. Charities should identify their substantial donors and take care and professional advice. In many cases, the type of transaction caught by the 2006 Act will be breach of trust and it will be clear that the charity should not enter into them (see 'The duty to apply the assets of the charity only for the charitable purposes within the charity's objects', page 155). However, the rules are widely drawn and may catch perfectly innocent transactions.

Legal and charity law issues relating to different types of corporate fundraising arrangements

Donations

Here, we are talking purely about gifts of money.

Gift Aid

To qualify for Gift Aid, donations must fulfil certain criteria:

- The gift must be a sum of money.

- There must not be any conditions as to repayment.

- In the case of individuals, the donor must make a Gift Aid declaration.

- The gift must not be associated with the donor or (any connected person) acquiring something.

- Any benefits received by the donor as a consequence of making the gift must not exceed the prescribed limits.

The prescribed limits are as follows:

Aggregate donations in the donor's tax year	Aggregate benefits in the donor's tax year
£0–£100	25% of value of donations
>£100–£1,000	£25
>£1,000	2.5% of value of donations, subject to maximum of £250

The word 'aggregate' is used in this table, because, when working out the value of the donations and connected benefits, what matters is the amount of all donations and benefits the donor receives in the whole year. If the benefits or donations are restricted to a period of less than 12 months, then the figures need to be adjusted pro rata. For more information on working this out, go to the HMRC's website.

A charity receives no extra tax benefit from a Gift Aid donation from a company; all the benefit goes to the donor company in the form of a deduction from its profits liable to corporation tax.

Gifts from sole traders or partners in a firm, by contrast, follow the Gift Aid rules for individuals (which include there being no prospect of the gift being returned and either no or very modest benefits to the donor). Gift Aid donations from individuals (including gifts from sole traders or partners in a firm) allow the charity to reclaim the basic rate of tax on donations. To claim the tax relief, the charity must make sure that individual donors make what is known as a Gift Aid declaration. This is a declaration by the donor that they want the charity to treat the gift as a Gift Aid donation. Declarations can be made in writing or over the telephone. For more detail on Gift Aid, declarations and including a link to some model wording see http://www.hmrc.gov.uk/charities/giftaid-charities/ declarations.htm

Companies with 'in-house' charities

Some companies have established 'in-house' charities. These vary in type but often the company will retain the right to appoint some or all of the trustees. Many companies with in-house charities only make donations to 'their' charity – referring all requests for grant and donations to the in-house charity.

Grants made by in-house charities, like those made by other charitable funders, do not come within the Gift Aid scheme (there is no tax reclaim that can be made by the recipient charity).

Payroll giving

Where a company or business runs a payroll giving scheme, its employees can ask their employer to deduct a sum from their pre-tax income, on a regular basis, and give it to the charity of their choice.

To run a payroll giving scheme an employer will need to enter a contract with an authorised payroll giving agency. A list of these agencies is available on the HMRC website. The employer pays the employees' contributions to the agency, which then sends the money on to the nominated charities.

There is no tax benefit to employers from running a payroll giving scheme – just good employee relations.

Charities do not have to do anything to take part in payroll giving schemes. They simply receive donations from the payroll giving agency.

Matched giving schemes

Many employers now run 'matched-giving schemes' in which employers agree to match (in whole or in part) whatever funds the employees pays or raise for charity, for example, by matching employee donations made through payroll giving.

A company's contribution under such a scheme is treated in the same way as a donation made outside such a scheme (it can deduct the donations from its pre-tax profits).

There are unlikely to be tax or legal issues for charities that benefit under these schemes, unless the employer intends advertising its scheme in such a way that it constitutes commercial participation. (See 'Commercial participation', below.)

Gifts in kind, including secondments

There are a number of tax reliefs available to companies that make gifts in kind to charities.

Gifts of land, building and shares

Companies can get tax relief when they make an outright gift to the charity but also when they sell property to the charity at less than its market value (at an undervalue). To qualify for the tax relief:

• Land and buildings must be freehold or leasehold properties in the UK and the company must transfer all of its interest in the property.

As regards shares, the relief only applies to:

- shares listed on a UK stock exchange or a recognised foreign stock exchange

- units in an authorised unit trust

- shares in a UK open-ended investment company

- holdings in certain foreign investment schemes.

It is the company that gets the benefit of tax benefits on such gifts and the way in which those benefits are calculated is beyond the scope of this book. However guidance is available on the HMRC website.

Before accepting a gift of land, buildings or shares, a charity needs to be satisfied that it has the necessary powers to accept and retain the gift. A charity will only be able to accept the property if it either has a suitable power of investment or, in the case of land, can use it to further its charitable purposes. Unincorporated charities will generally be able to accept land and shares, as they benefit from the wide investment powers in the Trustee Act 2000. Charitable companies will need to make sure they have suitable powers in their Memorandum and Articles.

If the charity has an appropriate power of investment to accept a gift of shares, it will still only be able to keep the shares if it considers that this would be an appropriate use of that power. There will be no tax or VAT implications if the charity decides to sell the shares.

The charity may be able to keep property, despite not having a power to invest in land, if it can use the land for its charitable purposes. If it cannot, then it will need to sell the land. In doing this, the charity must comply with the procedures the law requires them to undergo when selling charity land (these are in Section 36 ff of the Charities Act 1993).

If the charity cannot accept shares or land, it may ask the corporate donor to sell the asset and then give it the proceeds instead. The corporate donor will be able to give the proceeds under Gift Aid, as long as it meets the Gift Aid requirements (see 'Donations', above).

Gifts of equipment and trading stock

Where a business gives a charity:

- items that it makes or uses in the course of its business

- plant or machinery that it uses in the course of its business

it will get tax relief on the gift, in that it does not need to (as it would normally on giving away this type of property) treat the market value of the item as a trading receipt in its accounts.

From the charity's point of view, similar issues arise as with gifts of shares and land.

Secondment of staff by the company to the charity

The expenses incurred in making the secondment (including salary costs) are tax deductible by the company.

If the company is dealing with payment of the employee, then tax and national insurance issues should not arise for the charity. The charity will need to comply with the legislation relevant to its other staff, such as health and safety regulations.

As a general rule, the legal rights to intellectual property created by an employee belong to the employer – even if that employee is seconded to work for another body. Charities taking secondees should therefore take care to secure any intellectual property rights in secondees' work by an agreement with the company.

Commercial participation

This is the term used by the Charities Act 1992 to describe certain types of relationship between businesses and charities. The rules cover situations in which a business, in an advertising or sales campaign, says that it will give money to charity in connection with the sale of its goods and services. A classic example would be an advertisement for cornflakes that says '25p of every packet of Cornflakes will go to XYZ charity'.

If a company has already given money to charity and mentions this in a later advertising campaign, it may or may not be commercial participation, depending on the wording.

The charity thinking of entering into a commercial participation arrangement needs to consider whether it has the power to do so under its constitution (because it may be trading) and, if it has, whether it will be in the charity's interests to associate itself with the company and/or promotion in question.

The law requires the commercial participator to enter into a written agreement with the charity, before running its campaign. This agreement must contain the same details as an agreement with a professional fundraiser (see 'Using professional fundraisers', above). In addition, the agreement must, if the proceeds are to go to more than one charity, say what proportion each charity will get.

It is important for the charity to make sure it is clear what expenses the company can deduct from the proceeds, how it will deal with money before paying it to the charity and how often payments will be made. It will be better if the commercial participator is obliged to hold the money in a separate account, so that it does not get mixed up with the company's other funds.

Commercial participation may be a type of trading. If it is, and the charity expects the income from the venture to take it over the small trading limits, the venture will have to be run through a trading subsidiary. In this case, there will generally need to be a three-way agreement between the charity, the trading subsidiary and the commercial participator.

The law obliges a commercial participator to make a statement each time it makes a representation that it will give money to charity, in connection with a commercial participation arrangement. In broad terms, this statement must indicate what sums of money will go to charity. If the representation is made on radio or television and payments can be made by credit or debit card, the commercial participator must also make it clear that sums over £50 can be refunded, if the customer asks for a refund within seven days. Like the requirements for professional fundraisers, the content of the statements will change once Section 67 of the Charities Act 2006 is brought into force to refer to a 'notifiable amount'.

Brand licensing

A charity may decide (for example, as part of a commercial participation arrangement) to license its name and logo to a company.

There are several issues to consider here. As with any corporate link, the trustees of the charity will need to be satisfied that association with the company will be good for the charity.

If the trustees are happy that it will, then the charity will need to draw up a contract between the charity and the company. This contract will set out the ways in which the company may use the charity's logo and the payments that the company will make for it. To protect the charity's brand, the charity should ensure that the contract obliges the company to get the charity's prior approval for uses that are not specifically listed.

Brand licensing is not a charitable purpose, so entering into this type of agreement is generally regarded as taxable trading and, if the sums involved are large enough, usually routed through a subsidiary trading company. In some circumstances it is possible to change the tax treatment of the payment receivable by the charity by structuring the agreement so that the company is legally obliged to make an annual payment for use of the charity's logo.

Charities contemplating a licensing arrangement should always take professional advice.

Sponsorship

The term 'sponsorship' means arrangements whereby a company provides money to a charity in return for some recognition of its support. The recognition may range anything from a simple acknowledgment in related literature to a right to use the charity's logo or enjoy special privileges, such as an exclusive right to sell goods on the charity's premises.

If the sponsor decides, of its own accord, to exploit its connection with the charity, but without the charity itself having to do or give anything in return, then the sponsorship income can still be regarded as a donation and not as trading income. As a result, it will not be taxable.

Similarly, it is quite acceptable for the charity to include a small 'thank you' in its literature, provided the charity does not give the 'thank you' undue visibility or make large, prominent use of the sponsor's corporate colours or logo in the literature. In these circumstances, the sponsorship funding will again be seen as a donation.

If, on the other hand, the charity gives the sponsor a more prominent acknowledgement, or grants it special privileges, then the sponsorship money may be seen as payment for advertising or other services and taxable in the hands of the charity and liable to VAT. This may not matter to the corporate sponsor (as it may still be deductible from its pre-tax profits, as a trading expense and mopped up on its usual VAT reclaims), but from the charity's point of view it may be significant.

Sometimes sponsorship can be part of a primary purpose project and treated differently for tax purposes, for instance, if a company sponsors a production by a charitable theatre company and, in return, is allowed to put up a banner in the theatre lobby during the performances of the play. If the charitable theatre company is using the sponsorship income to produce the play, the sponsorship income may be tax-exempt (but great care is needed here because HMRC's attitude to such schemes appears to be hardening).

In many cases it will be sensible to split the agreed fee for a commercial sponsorship arrangement so that that part of the payment which represents 'value' for the sponsorship is treated as such and is separated from the balance of the payment, which can then be accepted as a donation. This is discussed briefly in 'The difference between donations and other arrangements', above.

HMRC website

www.gov.uk/charities/guidance-notes/

Template for a corporate fundraising strategy

Andrew Peel and Carla Miller

There has been much discussion about the importance of a clear, well-measured approach to developing a corporate fundraising strategy. This Appendix aims to condense these various strands and observations into an easily digestible format that can be used as a template or foundation for writing a strategy by any charity, regardless of its size and/or the level of corporate fundraising expertise.

Though the content and length of this section will naturally vary widely from one charity to another, the goal – to introduce and clearly set the scene for your work – should not. You should aim to outline the context in which your corporate fundraising is taking place and to highlight the fact that corporate fundraising cannot succeed if it is taking place in a vacuum.

Always endeavour to provide a full description of your team's work using clear, non-technical and jargon-free language. This is particularly important if the charity is new to corporate fundraising, since there is a greater chance that the reader will not fully appreciate the nature of your team or your fundraiser's work.

The broad areas you might address in the introduction include:

- a general outline of the organisation's aims

- an explanation of why the charity needs a corporate fundraising function

- an overview of how your strategy flows out of the wider fundraising strategy and the organisation's business plan

- a top-line description of your team's purpose, summary of current position, recent successes

'Articulating your vision'

How do you, as team leader, see the future for corporate fundraising? This is your opportunity to stamp your personal mark on the strategy, by conveying, in a few sentences, your overarching goal and focus.

Here's an example of a 'vision' for a larger charity:

'The Corporate Fundraising team will be generating £1.5m net by the end of 2012 – funding that will be secured through a combination of integrated, creative fundraising and marketing and by maximising the potential of local, regional, national and international corporate relationships.'

And for a smaller charity, something along these lines may be more appropriate:

'The Corporate Fundraising Team will continue to develop into a key fundraising and marketing function for the charity. We will double our net income over the next five years, from £175k to £350k as a result of investment in staff, by improving internal communications, by maximising the potential of the partnership with Acme plc, and by building a sustainable supporter-base of committed local and regional companies.'

Situational analysis

This section provides you with the opportunity to give more detail about your work, your team's strengths and vulnerabilities, your strategy and the key factors likely to impact upon your ability to deliver against your objectives over the short, medium and long term.

In your situational analysis, consider providing:

- an overview of the charity's positioning and USPs (unique selling propositions) in relation to corporate fundraising

- the key internal and external factors impacting upon your ability to fundraise from companies

- a more detailed description of the marketplace – the performance of key competitors, the advent of more 'strategic' company giving and less philanthropy, increased employee choice about charity adoptions

- a description of which types of corporate fundraising – donations, sponsorship, cause-related marketing, employee fundraising, volunteering, direct marketing campaigns – are working best for you, and why, and the areas in which you plan to invest during the next planning period

- a snapshot of the corporate supporters you have on your books, why they have bought into your organisation/cause, how you want to see those relationships developing and the companies or sectors you are planning to approach in the future

- a top-line financial analysis of your team's past performance with an explanation for the highs and lows, net and gross income, expenditure, return on investment, cash flow, percentage of repeat/reliable income, financial comparisons with your competitor charities, etc.

- a fuller analysis of your team or fundraiser's work, performance against targets and predictions and timings for the next planning period

- a summary of the outputs from strategic planning tools such as SWOT, Ansoff, Boston matrix, etc.

This would also be a sensible juncture to summarise all other critical timings, concerns and issues which you believe are likely to impact significantly upon both your team's work and/or your colleagues' own strategic plans and workload.

These may include, for example:

- the need for additional resources – e.g. to invest in new staff

- your wish for greater levels of support or buy-in from senior managers or trustees

- the importance of your team receiving good quality support from your communications/PR team

- the need for you to have access to appealing, corporate-friendly projects, better project information and good quality reports and case studies

- the quality of your database – or your need for one!

Setting clear objectives

These should provide an outline of your broad strategic direction.

A large charity's corporate fundraising strategy could, for instance, be built around core objectives such as:

1 'Maximise net income from community affairs budgets, "charity of the year" relationships, employee fundraising, payroll giving and other 'non-commercial' sources.'
2 'Better harness the power of the charity's brand by developing more "commercial" promotions, including cause-related marketing, sponsorship, licensing and affinity partnerships.'
3 'Maximise net income from, and professionally manage the development of, long-term, strategic and multi-faceted partnerships. Position the charity as a natural NGO partner for multinational companies.'
4 'Maximise corporate fundraising opportunities via closer collaboration with other fundraising colleagues. Work with community fundraising, trusts and the major donor team in order to develop a more proactive approach to networking, "peer-to-peer" fundraising and prospect cultivation.'
5 'Adopt a more sector-focused approach to corporate fundraising and new business. Research, approach and instigate dialogue with, for example, the banking sector, airlines, travel agents and other companies enjoying a natural synergy with our work.'

Next, outline the main actions required to carry out each of these objectives.

For example, if we elaborate on the first objective, we might see the following actions highlighted:

'Maximise net income from community affairs budgets, "charity of the year" relationships, employee fundraising, payroll giving and other 'non-commercial' sources.'

Action plan

• Continue to professionally manage and maximise the potential of existing relationships with X plc and Y Ltd.

• Recruit new account executive to support new business and sector-specific approaches (by end Qtr 1 2008).

• Continue to research and record charity of the year opportunities. Produce and manage timetable of approaches to warmest prospects.

• Recruit a new payroll giving manager by end of Qtr 2 2008.

• Build relationships with PFOs, payroll giving agencies and explore opportunities for local consortiums.

• Develop a regular programme of direct mailings to existing supporters and 'cold' companies.

• Develop a range of volunteering/skills exchange opportunities suitable for corporate partners' staff.

• Develop a 'bank' of companies willing to donate gifts in kind – e.g. computers, drugs, flights, freight, etc.

• Explore with auditors/head of finance whether gifts in kind can be classified as income.

• Research, develop and gain approval of the new ethical policy by end of Qtr 3 2008.

• Research corporate trusts and foundations. Manage timetable of approaches to best prospects.

A small charity's strategic objectives might focus on the following kinds of issues:

- The strategy for retaining, managing and developing your existing supporters, with clear outcomes and income targets given for each account.

- An overview of your new business strategy, with an explanation of your targets by industry/sector, size, location, propensity to support your kind of cause and proposed corporate fundraising mechanism.

- The need for additional investment in your team. This may be about recruiting an extra fundraiser, or highlighting the need for additional training for your current staff.

- The need for the charity to be ready to cope with the 'growing pains' and demands that a significant corporate partnership can place on a small organisation.

- Your wish to improve the marketing or packaging of your work, materials and funding opportunities.

- Networking – and how you intend to maximise the impact of senior internal contacts (e.g. your founder, directors, trustees and patrons) and other key colleagues (e.g. your major donor and events teams).

- The need to boost the charity's profile within the corporate world – e.g. via increased trade press and PR, reciprocal website links, a targeted direct mail campaign, a corporate networking event.

- Your perceived need for more challenge events to engage current and potential supporters.

- Your latest 'big ideas' – such as a quarterly 'corporate lunch with the chairman' event or the establishment of a corporate membership scheme or corporate supporters' panel.

Note: If objectives are set for a three- or five-year planning period, it is recommended that they be revisited annually as they can quickly date and lose their pertinence. A lot can change in the course of a year – particularly in a small charity!

You may also find it helpful to include a schedule or timetable of activity to simplify or clarify your plans.

Budgeting

The larger charity's five-year corporate fundraising budget could be presented as follows:

(× £100,000)	2008	2009	2010	2011	2012
General funds	750	825	950	1100	1300
Restricted funds	250	325	400	450	500
Trading income	50	50	75	100	125
Total income	1,050	1,200	1,425	1,650	1,925
Expenditure	150	225	300	350	425
Net contribution	900	975	1,125	1,300	1,500
Return on investment (ROI)	7:1	5.33:1	4.81:1	4.7:1	4.5:1

Sample commentary to support the budget:

'The fundraising budget reflects the priorities and restraints highlighted in this strategy – namely:

● the need to reduce our reliance on a small number of corporate donors and develop a wider range of sustainable income streams and fundraising 'products';

● the need to deliver growth both in general and restricted funds, with total budgeted net income increasing by 67 per cent over the 5-year period (from £900,00k to £1.5 million);

● the likely growth in restricted income (100 per cent increase 2008–12), reflecting the trend towards more project or product-based fundraising;

● the need to continue to build unrestricted marketing-led income (channelled via the trading company);

● the lead-in times (up to 1 year) necessary to secure many corporate partnerships;

● the need for new staff to be recruited and for the new team to 'bed in';

● the need to invest in this area of fundraising, whilst achieving acceptable ROIs.'

Much of the above can be amended to apply to small charities, too. However, when budgeting and forecasting be sure to address the following.

• Have you considered all potential income sources and expenditure? Carefully reappraise your plans and regular income streams, likely new sources, probability of success, phasing of donations and the impact of that phasing on cash flow.

• Have you developed a separate five-year financial forecast, highlighting predicted income growth, direct costs and investment costs?

• Have you made your financial targets as specific as possible – rather than – 'as much as possible'?

• Have you been conservative in your financial estimates? The best approach to setting fundraising income and expenditure targets is to under-promise and over-deliver!

Monitoring and evaluation

Fundraising strategies should be reviewed regularly – and modified as required – to ensure they are leading you towards your goals. It is important, therefore, for charities of all types and sizes to clarify the expected outcomes and be clear about what corporate fundraising success will look like at the end of set periods.

Your performance indicators or success measures could look like these.

Financial

• Increase in net income of x per cent per annum

• Minimum ROI of x:1 maintained throughout the strategic planning period

• Minimum of two new donors or partnerships secured per annum with a value of at least £x each

• Portfolio of committed corporate donors increasing by x per cent per annum – with X giving <£y per annum

• At least £x per annum generated by charity of the year relationships

- Payroll giving income increasing by x per cent and number of donors by y per cent per annum.

Operational

- Two additional corporate account executives recruited to support the delivery of the strategy

- x number of new charity of the year adoptions secured annually

- x number of marketing-led promotions agreed

- Improved range of 'products', campaigns and projects available for corporate support

- Annual survey suggests the charity's cultivation strategy and annual networking events have led to increased profile and awareness of our work amongst FTSE CEOs and key business groups

- The number of companies actively engaged in supporting our work is x – an increase of y per cent.

Qualitative

- A clearer and more motivational corporate case for support has been developed

- A more proactive and strategic approach to generating new business has been adopted

- Greater focus is now placed internally on securing and resourcing partnerships with companies

- Improvements have been made to internal communications and relationships with other departments, such as the operations team, finance

- Improvements made to the website mean a better online giving experience for corporate visitors

- Recruitment of x new fundraisers achieved; lower turnover of corporate fundraisers evident

- Industry award won by 2010.

An ethical framework for accepting or rejecting corporate support

Ian MacQuillin

Ethical decision-making frameworks can only be used as a guide to take you through some of the issues and questions that are at stake. They are not algorithms into which you plug a few variables and arrive at the ethically correct decision at the other end. An ethical decision-making framework is not the same as a professional code of best practice.

This ethical decision-making framework (and indeed any such framework you use) *must* be used in conjunction with the Institute of Fundraising (IoF) codes of practice on the Acceptance and Refusal of Donations, and Charities Working with Business.

1 Identify that there is – or may be – an ethical issue

For instance:

• Does the company's core business area conflict with your cause or service delivery (for instance, if you are a cancer charity and they are a tobacco company)?

• Does the company have a history of public controversy or negative media coverage?

• Does it work in an area that you or your staff consider problematic or unethical?

• Is it in financial difficulty?

2 Identify and list your objections, if any, to the offer of support

Have you understood the difference between consequentialist and deontological ethics? (See Chapter 7.) Decide whether your objections are consequentialist (it would be detrimental for your charity to work with this company) or deontological (it would be 'wrong' for your charity to work with this company) – or a mix of the two – and list them separately.

For instance (C = consequentialist; D = deontological):

• The company is an arms company and I do not want to work with people that make weapons (D)

• The company is an arms company that has recently been accused in the press of supplying outlawed anti-personnel devices (D + C)

• When we last partnered a defence company, several major donors withdrew their support and it took us two years to get our major donor income back to a comparable level (C)

• Most of the fundraisers in the department have heard that the company exploits its workers in the Philippines (D)

• Although we are a children's charity, this company conducts animal experiments and we can't be seen to be supporting or endorsing such practices (D)

• We are a homelessness charity and this house-building company wants to secure planning permission to build on green land and we think it is using us as part of its PR offensive (C)

3 Test the objections

Run each objection through the 'filter' of the IoF code of practice on accepting or rejecting donations. Is each objection independent of:

• individual or personal opinions

• political or commercial interests

• your personal moral position

…which are not directly related to the charity?

If you have allowed the ethical objection to be swayed by any of these conditions, then reformulate the objection to take this into account. If you cannot, you must ditch the objection. For instance, if you do not want to accept money from an arms company, that is a personal choice that does not survive the acceptance/rejection filter.

For each separate objection that survives the filter, decide how, if you acted on this objection and refused the offer of support, you would be able to justify this to the Charity Commission as having acted 'in the best interests of the charity'.

This means that for each of your listed objections, you will need to compile evidence to support your assertion that rejecting the offer of support is 'in the best interests of the charity'.

To do this you will need to get the facts about the company:

- business practices

- financial state

- CSR practices

- what it wants out of the corporate partnership

- a thorough understanding of problematic ethical issues.

See Section 2.4 of the IoF code of practice (Charities Working with Business).

Does this knowledge about the company undermine any of your objections?

For instance, what if most of your fundraisers believe that the company operates an unethical third world supply chain, but endorsement from third party social responsibility monitoring organisations refutes this. Note that if this is the case, even if your fundraisers still believe the *status quo ante*, then the objection is still undermined because the correct ethical decision is not dependent on what your staff erroneously believe to be true but on what actually is true.

You will then need to test your ethical objections. To do this you will need to do one, some or all of the following:

Ask your donors

Ask your donors how their support or giving would be affected were you to accept the offer of corporate support. If you believe that your donors will stop giving but your market research shows that they don't care at all about this company supporting you, then your (consequentialist) objection is undermined.

(This research must be open, honest and scientific, based on a statistically robust sample. If it has been designed to elicit certain responses to support your prejudiced decision to reject a donation, then you would be allowing your personal view to influence the decision, in contravention of the IoF code of practice. In any event, it is unethical to fake scientific research.)

Ask your beneficiaries

Ask your beneficiaries whether they would want you to accept the decision. As a fundraiser you have a responsibility to respect the dignity of your beneficiaries. If they do not wish you to associate with a particular company, you have strong – almost overwhelming – evidence that rejecting that support is in the best interest of the charity's core stakeholder group. In fact, 'our beneficiaries don't want it', is about the strongest defence you could have. On the other side of the coin, so is 'our beneficiaries want it'.

There is a difference in the questions you ask your donors and beneficiaries. With donors, you are assessing the possible consequences of accepting corporate support. You should not ask your existing donors whether you *should* accept that support, because their views on this are not relevant. This is a question that you should direct to your beneficiaries.

Do *not* ask your staff, either fundraisers or the whole charity. The views of staff are not relevant in determining whether an issue at hand is ethical or unethical. Ethical correctness is not derived by majority vote.

Previous partnerships

Look at how similar corporate partnerships (with this company, with your charity and with similar charities and companies) have played out in the past. Is there anything you can learn that might inform your course of action?

PR risk assessment

Conduct a media risk assessment to assess the likelihood, extent and consequences of negative media coverage.

4 After you have made a decision:

a) Ensure that you can make a consistent justification. Do not switch from consequentialist to deontological justifications and back again. If you turn down a donation from a company that conducts animal experimentation because you fear negative media coverage and then pretend you did so because animal experimentation is morally 'wrong' (even though you are a, say, children's charity), then you will end up tying yourself in philosophical knots as you try publicly to make a deontological defence of a consequentialist position.

b) Monitor how it plays out. If you find that your donors do in fact desert you in droves, then you have reason, and a responsibility, to end the relationship, if it is no longer in the best interest of the charity to do so. However, the commercial participator agreement you sign with the company *must* allow you get-out clauses if certain outcomes result.

c) The ultimate justification: if you came face to face with one of your beneficiaries or an inspector from the Charity Commission, would you be able to say to them, hand on heart, that you made the best decision for the charity?

Sources for corporate information

Robin Jones

This appendix provides some of the best free and pay-to-view sites on the web. There are plenty of sources of information out there on companies, some very expensive, others free. Information on stock market listed companies is readily available, as they are obliged by law to provide you with a copy of their annual report. Data on limited companies is harder to obtain and usually comes at a price, but there are a number of websites that offer you free basic information with further details being available on a pay-per-view basis. Online subscription sites can be expensive but most will provide trials and online demonstrations of their products, giving you a chance to evaluate them.

• www.boardex.com/nfp.aspx – BoardEx is the trading name of Management Diagnostics, a privately owned corporate research company. BoardEx helps identify and track potential donors among corporate board members.

• www.bvdep.com/ – Bureau van Dijk has a range of subscription-based online databases covering the corporate world. DASH is a database of UK companies, directors and shareholders. FAME is a database that contains information on 3.4 million companies in the UK and Ireland.

• www.carol.co.uk – Carol is an online service offering direct links to the financial pages of listed companies in Europe and the USA. It provides direct access to company balance sheets, profit and loss statements, financial highlights, etc.

• www.chambersandpartners.com – Guides to law firms and lawyers in the UK.

• www.cityoflondon.gov.uk/corporation/leisure_heritage/libraries_ archives_museums_galleries/city_london_libraries/cbl.htm – City Business Library, located in Moorgate, London. An excellent resource providing free access to business information such as company annual reports, financial data and market research.

• www.companieshouse.gov.uk – Free access to basic information on all UK listed companies. Subscription service allows you to download director details and full company accounts.

- Directory of Social Change's subscription site – www.companygiving. org.uk A database of company support available to voluntary and community organisations. Contains details on around 500 companies and is also available in book and CD formats.

- www.corporateregister.co.uk/ – This quarterly publication, produced by HS Financial Publishing, contains information on every one of the UK's 2,000 quoted companies, on 14,000 senior executives and 1,800 professional advisers. Includes biographical information on the directors as well as their remuneration.

- www.corporatewatch.org.uk – Corporate Watch is a small independent not-for-profit research and publishing group that undertakes research on the social and environmental impact of large corporations, particularly multinationals. The website also has a good guide to research companies

- www.dnb.com/kbe/ – Key British Enterprises. This database provides you with the facts about the corporate background, activities, decision-makers, finances, operations and markets of Britain's leading businesses. Search by region or industry.

- www.eiris.org/ – EIRIS is the leading global provider of independent research into the social, environmental and ethical performance of companies. A UK-based organisation with an office in the USA and a representative office in Japan, its international research partners together have a wealth of experience in the field of socially responsible investment (SRI) research. It provides comprehensive research on more than 2,800 companies in Europe, North America and Asia Pacific.

- www.factiva.co.uk – Factiva®, a Dow Jones & Reuters company, provides business news and financial information from over 10,000 sources.

- www.freebizinfo.org/ – An excellent guide to free corporate information from the Association for Information Management (Aslib).

- www.hemscott.com/ – A provider of UK company information providing free service financial information on 2,350 UK and Irish listed companies. Hemscott.com contains financial data taken from Annual Reports and Company Announcements, ratios, executive and non-executive directors, the latest Regulatory News (RNA), email news and price alerts, latest results and company key dates. Hemscott also publishes the Directory of Directors, profiling over 50,000 directors and officers and 12,000 companies.

- www.hollis-publishing.com/ – Hollis produces a number of guides, including: the *Hollis UK PR Annual,* a guide to PR consultancies, their clients and thousands of in-house spokespeople in the UK; *Hollis Europe*, with information on over 3,000 PR consultancies and 1,000 in-house PR contacts within 37 European countries, also includes public affairs, government relations, EU specialists and European sponsorship specialists; *Advertisers Annual*, with information on 3,000 advertising agencies and the UK's 2,000 top spending advertisers across 120 industry sectors; *Hollis Sponsorship & Donations Yearbook*, a guide to the UK's top sponsoring and donating companies, plus sponsorship opportunities, specialist sponsorship consultancies and services.

- www.icc.co.uk – Specialises in providing in-depth business information on all UK and Irish companies, including private companies, and their directors and shareholders as well as European and international companies.

- www.jordans.co.uk – This company produces JordanWatch, an online database and search service, for UK company information. You can access basic details on over 2 million limited companies at no cost.

- www.kellysearch.co.uk/ – A comprehensive database of UK and companies. Search by product and location.

- www.kompass.co.uk – Kompass produces a database of 1.9 million companies in over 70 countries. Search by company name, sector or region. Basic searches are free.

- www.lexisnexis.co.uk – LexisNexis have a number of online subscription services including LexisNexis Executive, a database of approximately 12,000 publications from national and local newspapers, press releases, transcripts of television broadcasts, newswires, statistical bulletins, magazines and trade journals.

- w.londonstockexchange.com – Detailed information on all UK and international companies quoted on the stock market. The site also has a free downloadable spreadsheet of the complete list of UK, international and AIM companies currently listed on the Stock Exchange at: www.londonstockexchange.com/en-gb/about/statistics/

- www.majorcompanies.co.uk/ – Provides free information on the top 100 companies in a wide range of company sectors.

- www.marketingfile.com – Access to a wide range of company lists. You can access by locality, sector and size. Pay per number of prospects.

- www.newsco.com/ – A leading independent publisher of business information. Produces Business Insider, a series of regional guides to companies and their owners, as well as regional rich lists. Back issues can be ordered from their website.

- www.northcote.co.uk/ – Provides easy and free access to UK company annual reports on the Internet.

- www.thomsonbusinessintelligence.com – An easy-to-use online news database that is one of the largest sources of news on companies, both international and national.

Also on corporate social responsibility:

- www.accountability21.net – Institute of Social and Ethical AccountAbility

- www.accountabilityrating.com – Accountability Rating TM

- www.bitc.org.uk – Business in the Community

- www.cepaa.org – Social Accountability International – SA 8000

- www.ftse4good.co.uk – FTSE4Good

- www.globalreporting.org – Global Reporting Initiative

- www.oecd.org – Organisation for Economic Co-operation and Development

- www.unglobalcompact.org – United Nations Global Compact

Other publications from the Directory of Social Change

All the following titles are published by the Directory of Social Change, unless otherwise stated, and are available from:

DSC Books
Directory of Social Change
24 Stephenson Way
London
NW1 2DP

Call 08450 77 77 07 or e-mail publications@dsc.org.uk for more details and a free publications list, which can also be viewed on the DSC website (www.dsc.org.uk).

The fundraising series

Published in association with the Charities Aid Foundation and the Institute of Fundraising.

Major Donor Fundraising
Margaret M Holman
Lucy Sargent

Funding from wealthy donors can mean the different between a charity's success or failure, yet many don't set aside the time or resources to find and build relationships with the people whose financial support matters the most. Illustrated with comprehensive case studies and real-life examples from both the UK and the US, this book offers practical, step-by-step advice about how to go about getting – and, most importantly, keeping, major gift donors. It will show you how to:

- identify key benefactors
- develop a fundraising strategy
- cultivate your most promising contacts
- make the all-important 'ask'
- create a culture that values major donors.

Written by experienced fundraising professionals, this guide is essential reading for anyone who wants to improve the fundraising prospects of their voluntary or social enterprise organisation.

196 pages, 1st edition, 2006, ISBN 978 1 903991 68 8

Capital Campaigns
Trudy Hayden

Capital campaigns require precisely defined, tightly structured fundraising strategies that can radically improve the fundraiser's chances of success, yet smaller organisations often lack the resources to hire specialists to manage their campaigns for them. This new guide gives the fundraiser, the CEO, the trustees and other management staff the information necessary to run a successful capital campaign – with or without a consultant's input.

Drawing upon her experience planning and managing several highly visible and successful campaigns, the author first defines what a capital campaign is, before going through each stage of their preparation and execution, including:

- the decision to run a campaign
- establishing goals for your campaign
- preparing strategies
- post-campaign tactics.

128 pages, 1st edition, 2006, ISBN 978 1 903991 62 6

Fundraising Strategy
Redmond Mullin

The key to successful fundraising is rigorous strategic planning and this influential title has become essential reading for all serious fundraisers, as a background to the whole series. The second edition draws on some more recent examples, such as the NSPCC Full Stop campaign, to further clarify the principles and process of strategy and demonstrate its place in fundraising campaigns. The book:

- discusses the concept of strategy and its relevance to not-for-profit bodies
- outlines the planning process for designing and implementing the strategy
- provides case studies of different strategies in different types and sizes of funding programmes

- has been fully updated to take into account important changes in areas such as the tax regime and the National Lottery.

160 pages, 2nd edition, 2002 ISBN 978 1 903991 22 0

Community Fundraising
Edited by Harry Brown

Volunteer networks are a key resource for fundraising, but are often not appreciated as they should be. This new title demonstrates how to make the most of your volunteers. It covers:

- what community fundraising is
- why people volunteer, the value of volunteers and staff attitudes to volunteers
- the recruitment, retention and development of volunteers
- the management of staff working with volunteers
- case studies from a range of different types of charities – and what can be learned from these.

192 pages, 1st edition, 2002 ISBN 978 1 900360 98 2

Fundraising Databases
Peter Flory

Computerised databases are an essential tool for fundraising, but fundraisers often lack the technical background to help them choose a suitable database and use it effectively. This new book provides a clear framework for making and implementing such decisions. It explains what a database is and how it works, before going on to examine:

- why fundraisers need a database
- the functions of a fundraising database
- future trends.

Case studies from a range of charities are used throughout to illustrate the points made.

160 pages, 1st edition, 2001 ISBN 978 1 900360 91 3

Legacy Fundraising
The Art of Seeking Bequests
Edited by Sebastian Wilberforce

This unique guide to one of the most important sources of revenue for charities has been revised and updated to include new material on telephone fundraising, forecasting income, and profiling. It also contains the full text of the new Institute of Fundraising Code of Practice on legacy fundraising. Contributions from a range of experts in the field cover both strategy and techniques, and are complemented by perspectives from donors and their families. The breadth of coverage and accessible style ensure that, whether you are an established legacy fundraiser or new to the field, this book is a must.

224 pages, 2nd edition, 2001 ISBN 978 1 900360 93 7

Trust Fundraising
Edited by Anthony Clay

This book outlines a variety of approaches to trusts that will save trustees' time and ensure greater success for fundraising by:

- emphasising the importance of research and maintaining records
- demonstrating the value of using contacts and a personal approach
- reinforcing the need for detailed planning of a strategy
- showing how to make an approach to trusts, and how not to
- stressing the importance of continued contact with a trust.

152 pages, 1st edition, 1999 ISBN 978 1 85934 069 1

Marketing Strategy
For Effective Fundraising
Peter Maple

A well thought out marketing strategy plays a key role in successful fundraising, from the largest to the smallest voluntary organisation.

Drawing upon the author's own practical experiences and illustrating those of other relevant experts, this book offers a down-to-earth guide to effective marketing including:

- drawing on and building upon appropriate commercial marketing practices
- identifying the vital elements of marketing strategy

- using the concept of 'brand value' to strengthen and focus communications
- realising the enormous marketing potential of an organisation's volunteers
- keeping abreast of twenty-first century media developments
- understanding the implications of future developments in marketing opportunities.

168 pages, 1st edition, 2003 ISBN 978 1 903991 38 1

Other fundraising titles from DSC

DSC publishes a range of other fundraising titles, including both directories and practical guides. Biennial directories include *A Guide to the Major Trusts* (volumes 1 and 2), *The Educational Grants Directory*, *The Guide to Grants for Individuals in Need* and *The Guide to UK Company Giving*. All titles can be ordered online (www.dsc.org.uk/charitybooks.html) or by calling 08450 77 77 07.

We also host three subscription-based fundraising websites: *trustfunding. org.uk*, *grantsforindividuals.org.uk* and *companygiving.org.uk*. Information is taken from all the major directories, and is constantly updated.

About the Directory of Social Change

DSC's vision is of an independent voluntary sector at the heart of social change. DSC has three objectives:

- To help voluntary organisations become effective agents for social change through the provision of support through training, publishing, networks, information and research.

- To promote independence for the sector by campaigning for an independent voluntary sector and championing the needs of small- to medium-sized voluntary and community organisations.

- To maintain independence, and consequently an independent voice, through being predominantly self-funded.

DSC publishes an extensive range of guides, handbooks and CD-ROMs, covering subjects such as fundraising, management, communication, finance and law. DSC has a range of subscription-based websites containing a wealth of information on funding from trusts and companies. DSC runs conferences and more than 350 courses each year.

For details of all our activities, and to order publications and book training courses, go to www.dsc.org.uk, call 08450 777707 or e-mail publications@dsc.org.uk

The Directory of Social Change
24 Stephenson Way
London
NW1 2DP

Federation House
Hope Street
Liverpool
L1 9BW

About the Charities Aid Foundation

The Charities Aid Foundation (CAF) is a registered charity with a unique mission – to increase the substance of charity in the UK and overseas. It provides services that are both charitable and financial which help donors make the most of their giving and charities make the most of their resources.

As an integral part of its activities, CAF works to raise standards of management in voluntary organisations. This includes the making of grants by its own Grants Council, sponsorship of the Charity Annual Report and Accounts Awards, seminars, training courses and its own Annual Conference, the largest regular gathering of key people from within the voluntary sector. In addition, CAF is recognised as a leading exponent of the internet for all those with an interest in charitable activity.

For decades, CAF has led the way in developing tax-effective services to donors, and these are now used by more than 250,000 individuals and 2,000 of the UK's leading companies, between them giving £150 million each year to charity. Many are also using CAF's unique range of investment and administration services for charities includes the CafCash High Interest Cheque Account, three specialist investment funds for longer-term investment and a full appeals and subscription management service.

CAF's activities are not limited to the UK, however. Increasingly, CAF is looking to apply the same principles and develop similar services internationally, in its drive to increase the substance of charity across the world. CAF has offices and sister organisations in the United States, South Africa, Russia, India and Brussels.

CAF Research is a leading source of information and research on the voluntary sector's income and resources. Its annual publication, *Dimensions of the Voluntary Sector*, provides year-on-year updates and its Research Report series covers a wide range of topics, including costs benchmarking, partnership resources, and trust and company funding. More details on research and publications may be found on www.CAFonline.org/research

For more information about CAF, please visit www.CAFonline.org/

About the Institute of Fundraising

The Institute of Fundraising (IOF) is the professional membership body for fundraisers, working to develop, promote and champion excellence in UK fundraising. Committed to the highest standards in fundraising practice and management, the Institute is the leading representative voice for fundraising. The Institute works to shape policy and influence legislation, engaging with charities, Government, media, the general public, and other relevant bodies across a broad spectrum of issues that impact UK fundraising.

The Institute strives to support and develop the knowledge and standards of all those who undertake fundraising and has an extensive range of training and networking opportunities. The Institute's Certificate in Fundraising Management is the leading qualification for fundraisers and is delivered by accredited training providers across the country.

The Institute offers an extensive programme of events. The flagship event, the National Convention, is the largest fundraising event of its type outside the USA, attracting around 2,000 charity representatives of all levels: CEOs, fundraisers, marketing and communication professionals, and policy advisers. The three-day programme is supplemented by a series of targeted one-day fundraising conferences taking place throughout the year.

As a membership body, the Institute represents over 4,000 fundraisers and 200 fundraising organisations, providing a wide range of information and support services for Individual and Organisational members. Individual membership supports fundraisers in providing tools that help them fundraise more effectively, opportunities to discuss common issues, as well as professional development support and advice. Organisational membership is an organisation-wide commitment to best practice in fundraising and provides a fast-track route to effect change in the UK fundraising environment.

Membership benefits include a free subscription to *Third Sector* magazine, the Codes of Fundraising Practice, a monthly email briefing covering key fundraising issues, access to a free legal helpline (provided by Bircham Dyson Bell), substantial discount packages on training and networking events including the Institute's flagship event – the National Convention.

The Institute is represented across the UK by a range of national, regional and special-interest groups, offering an extensive programme of networking and training events.

Institute of Fundraising Codes of Fundraising Practice and Code of Conduct

The Institute of Fundraising's Codes of Fundraising Practice set out the best practice standards for fundraisers operating within the UK. Each Code covers a separate fundraising technique or issue, as well as an overarching Code of Conduct setting out the framework of ethical behaviour for fundraisers. The Codes provide not only information on relevant areas of the law but outline recommended practice based upon the highest standards of fundraising.

All 4,000 Individual and 200 Organisational members of the Institute have already committed to meet the best practice guidance outlined within the Codes. The Codes are the best practice criteria upon which the forth-coming self-regulatory scheme for fundraising is built.

The Codes are drawn up by working parties composed of represen-tatives of the various interested constituents in a particular field, and undergo an extensive consultation process through the charities affiliated with the Institute of Fundraising, regulators and Government. As new areas of interest are identified, so new Codes are drafted, under the supervision of the Institute of Fundraising Standards Committee.

Codes of Fundraising Practice

Acceptance and Refusal of Donations
Accountability and Transparency
Best Practice for Fundraising Contracts
Best Practice for Major Donor Fundraising
Charity Challenge Events
Charities Working with Business
Committed Giving in the Workplace
Data Protection
Event Fundraising
Face-to-Face Fundraising (on the street and house-to-house)
Fundraising from Grant-MakingTrusts
Fundraising in Schools
Fundraising through Electronic Media
Handling of Cash Donations

House-to-House Collections
Legacy Fundraising
Management of Static Collection Boxes
Outdoor Fundraising in the UK
Payment of Fundraisers on a Commission Basis
Raffles and Lotteries
Reciprocal Charity Mailing
Scottish Charity Law in Relation to Fundraising and Public Charitable
Collections in Scotland
Telephone Fundraising
Telephone Recruitment of Collectors
Use of Chain Letters as a Fundraising Technique
Volunteer Fundraising

Guidance

Guidance for 'In Aid Of' Volunteer Fundraisers
Model Contracts and Standard Forms of Agreement

New Codes for 2007

Best Practice for Fundraising Consultants
Direct Mail
Revised Legacy Code

Copies of the Codes of Practice and Code of Conduct can be downloaded from the Institute of Fundraising's websites:

www.institute-of-fundraising.org.uk

For further information please contact the Policy Team Institute of Fundraising at:

Institute of Fundraising
Park Place
12 Lawn Lane
London
SW8 1UD

Tel: 020 7840 1046
Fax: 020 7840 1001

Email: codes@institute-of-fundraising.org.uk

Index

AA1000 framework 16–17, 18
Accountability Rating™ 14, 18, 19
ActionAid 54–5
adoption *see* 'charity of the year'
  schemes; partnership working
advertising *see* cause-related
  marketing; public relations (PR)
application processes 35–7, 97–101,
  145–7
  case studies 83–4, 109–15

BAE Systems case study 109–15
Barclays 10, 21
benchmarking 9, 18, 79, 85
  Corporate Responsibility (CR)
    index 79, 85
  London Benchmarking Group
    (LBG) 9, 49–55, 85 *see also*
    standards/measures for corporate
    social responsibility
beneficiaries 63–4, 186–7
'best endeavours' clauses 166
BIBIC/IPC Media case study 144–50
bidding processes 35–7, 97–101,
  145–7
  case studies 83–4, 109–15
brand licensing, legal matters 173
  see also cause-related marketing
Breakthrough Breast Cancer 8, 10
  partnership with Marks & Spencer
    116–22
budgets, fundraising 181–2
business analysis tools 39–40, 176–7
Business in the Community 5, 7, 25,
  33, 55, 78
  Corporate Responsibility (CR)
    index 79, 85

cause-related marketing 8, 20, 25–7
  brand licensing 173

case studies 71–6, 86–92, 106–8,
  116–22, 138
  history 3–6
  legal and tax issues 172–4
charitable foundations ('in-house'
  charities) 20, 169
  Tomorrow's People Trust 5–6, 54
Charities Aid Foundation (CAF) 4, 27,
  31, 49
Charity Commission, guidance on
  duties of trustees 59, 64, 154–7
charity law 154–74
'charity of the year' schemes 8, 23–5,
  32 *see also* partnership working
  case studies 83–4, 109–15, 123–32,
    144–50
Citizens' Advice Bureau/EDF
  partnership 82
collaboration with other charities 28,
  46, 99, 163
commercial participation 172–4
communication, importance of 22, 27,
  74, 84, 91, 96, 120, 128–9, 142,
  148
community investment 3–11, 21–2,
  78–85 *see also* types of CI
  e.g. employees, cause-related
  marketing, gifts in kind
companies
  researching 23–4, 30–1, 98–9, 110,
    163–4
  approaching/applying to 35–7,
    83–4, 97–101, 109–15, 145–7
  developing relationships with 30–7,
    38–46, 73–5, 90–1, 97–102,
    116–22, 133–43
conflicts of interest 58, 104, 156–7,
  161
contacts, building 31–2, 41, 45, 96,
  97–102

contracts 74, 164–7, 172
core funding (vs. project funding) 8–9,
    21–2
Corporate Citizenship Company 49,
    55
corporate fundraisers
    recruiting 144
    role 31–7
    team structures 42–6, 90, 95–7, 142
    TreeHouse case study 93–102
corporate partners *see* companies;
    partnership working
Corporate Responsibility (CR) index
    79, 85
corporate social responsibility (CSR)
    12–20, 31, 33–4, 38, 140
    case studies 77–85, 145
    consultants 33–4
    reporting/standards 7, 14–19, 79,
    85
customer relationship management
    (CRM) databases 44–5, 96

databases, fundraising 44–5, 96
Diabetes UK case study 103–8
Diageo (Grand Metropolitan) 5–6, 54
donors
    business types 162–3
    donor cultivation cycle, seven-step
    97
    donor-led corporate fundraising case
    study 93–102
    major donors 167–8

EDF Energy case study 77–85
employees (company)
    fundraising 22–5, 123–32 *see also*
    'charity of the year' schemes
    payroll giving schemes 8, 23, 27–8,
    170
    secondments 172
    volunteering 7–8, 28–9, 83–4,
    109–10, 113
environment, impacts on *see* corporate
    social responsibility (CSR); EDF
    case study
ethics 46, 57–65, 184–7
    Diabetes UK case study 103–8
evaluation and monitoring 22, 47–56,
    85, 129–32, 149–50, 182–3
events 33, 90

'fit' of organisations 117, 133–4,
    140–1
Foundation for the Study of Infant
    Deaths (FSID) case study 69–76
fundraisers
    employed by charities 31–7, 42–6,
    90, 93–102, 95–7, 142, 144
    professional fundraisers (external
    organisations) 28, 166–7

Gift Aid 162, 168–9 *see also* tax
gifts in kind 9–10, 29, 53, 170–2
    InKind Direct 9
Give As You Earn (GAYE) *see* payroll
    giving schemes
Global Compact, United Nations
    15–16
Global Reporting Initiative 17–18
gro-group®/FSID partnership 71–6

HBOS case study 123–32
'heads of agreement' 164
history
    corporate community investment
    3–11
    corporate social responsibility (CSR)
    12–20
'hooks' (getting a company interested)
    32, 33

impacts, measuring 36–7, 48, 52–4
    EDF case study 77–85
'in-house' charities 20, 169
    Tomorrow's People Trust 5–6, 54
in kind support 9–10, 29, 53, 170–2
    InKind Direct 9
Institute of Fundraising, code of
    practice on ethical fundraising
    58–61, 64, 185–6
IPC Media/BIBIC partnership 144–50
ISO
    14000 series 14–15
    26000 series 16

lawyers, using 164–6
legal issues 154–74
leverage 5–6, 48, 52–4, 136, 138,
    147
licensing, brand 173 *see also*
    cause-related marketing
logos *see* cause-related marketing

London Benchmarking Group (LBG) 9, 49–55, 85
long-term partnerships, UNICEF/ Manchester Utd case study 133–43

major donors 167–8
Manchester United/UNICEF partnership 133–43
marketing *see* cause-related marketing; public relations (PR)
Marks & Spencer 3, 10
  Breakthrough Breast Cancer partnership 116–22
matched funding schemes 83, 170
Mencap/EDF partnership 82–4
monitoring and evaluation 22, 47–56, 85, 129–32, 149–50, 182–3
moral issues *see* ethics
mutual benefit 6, 18–20, 21–9, 36, 90–1

networks, maximising existing 32, 41, 45, 97–102

objectives 178–80
  measuring 47–56
OECD Declaration 15
on-pack promotions *see* cause-related marketing
output/impacts reporting 36–7, 48, 52–4

Pareto principle 41
partnership working 6, 10–11, 24–5, 30–7, 38–46
  BIBIC/IPC Media 144–50
  Breakthrough Breast Cancer/Marks & Spencer 116–22
  CAB/EDF 82
  Diabetes UK/Morrisons 106–8
  FSID/gro-group" 71–6
  Mencap/EDF 82–4
  RNLI/Wall's 86–92
  UNICEF/Manchester United 133–43
  Wildlife Trusts/EDF 81
partnerships (firms), accepting donations from 162–3
payroll giving schemes 8, 23, 27–8, 170
PerCent model 7

personal contacts 31–2, 41, 45, 96, 97–102
pitching processes 35–7, 97–101, 145–7
  case studies 83–4, 109–15
power balances 10, 26–7, 163–4
presentations 102, 110–15, 146
  see also pitching processes
professional fundraisers 28, 166–7
ProHelp 7–8
project funding (vs. core funding) 8–9, 21–2
project results (outputs), focus on 36–7, 48, 52–4
promotions *see* cause-related marketing
proposals, written 35 *see also* pitching processes
public relations (PR)
  agencies 34
  departments (company) 31
  resources (charity) 30, 36, 45

relationships with companies, developing 32, 33–5, 38–46, 97–102
  case studies 73–5, 90–1, 116–22, 133–43
researching corporate partners 23–4, 30–1, 98–9, 110, 163–4
resources, gifts of *see* gifts in kind
risk assessments 60, 80
RNLI/Wall's partnership 86–92

SA8000 17
Sainsbury's 3, 4, 9–10
secondments 9–10, 172 *see also* gifts in kind
selling goods 157–61, 173
seven-step donor cultivation cycle 97
Shell 13, 20
situational analysis 39–40, 176–7
small and medium-sized enterprises (SME) 46
smaller charities 46
  BIBIC case study 144–50
  FSID case study 69–76
social return on investment (SROI) 54
society, impacts on *see* corporate social responsibility (CSR)

sponsorship 6, 174 *see also*
    cause-related marketing; 'charity
    of the year' schemes; partnership
    working
stakeholders 12, 18–20, 22, 36, 56,
    79, 142 *see also* beneficiaries
standards/measures for corporate
    social responsibility (CSR) *see
    also* benchmarking
    AA1000 framework 16–17
    Accountability RatingTM 14, 18, 19
    Global Compact, United Nations
        15–16
    Global Reporting Initiative 17–18
    ISO 26000 series 16
    OECD Declaration 15
    PerCent model 7
    SA8000 17
    United Nations Global Compact
        15–16
steering groups 22, 25
strategic partnerships 21
strategic planning for corporate
    fundraising 38–46, 99
strategic analysis 39–40, 176–7
template strategic plan 175–83
subsidiary trading companies 160–1
substantial donors 167–8
supporter events 33

tax 167–8, 170–4
    trading 158–61
Tomorrow's People Trust 5–6, 54
trading 157–61, 173
TreeHouse case study 93–102
trustees
    duties of 59, 64, 154–7
    using as contacts 32, 41, 45, 96

UNICEF/Manchester United
    partnership 133–43
United Nations Global Compact
    15–16

v (youth volunteering charity) 11
VAT 159, 160, 174
vision, articulating 39, 79, 176
Vodafone 21, 53, 138
volunteering (employees) 7–8, 28–9,
    113
    BAE Systems' Charity Challenge
        109–10
    EDF case study 83–4
    ProHelp 7–8

Wildlife Trusts/EDF partnership 81